10 GREAT WINE FAMILIES

A tour through Europe

10 GREAT WINE FAMILIES

A tour through Europe

Fiona Morrison MW

Photography by Alexandre James Rocca-Serra

Foreword – Hugh Johnson

I often think it is a little miracle when I read 'X & Son' on a shopfront, a bigger one when it says 'X & Sons', and a tall story when a business claims to have cascaded down many generations without a hitch.

Nothing relating to wine is straightforward either. There are warning signs every step of the way. Few industries involve so many crucial decisions, from what to plant that will endure for half a century to when to pick when an anticyclone looms over the Azores. From how to pick and sort the grapes, transport them, crush them, macerate them in what sort of vessel, with stems or not – and for how long. Barrels or not? Which oak? ...to the question of how much to charge.

However well families get on as individuals, the strains of doing business together are obvious, and when doing wine business, quite scary. Then there is the problem of inheritance: rarely easy, especially with the state taking a hand in the matter.

Fiona Morrison has written a book from a viewpoint no other writer, as far as I know, has ever possessed: a seat at the heart of this action. She is a Master of Wine who belongs to one of Bordeaux's most successful families. Yet she manages to be remarkably dispassionate about this family and its doings, including how it makes what all agree is very great wine. In choosing to portray through her interviews 10 of the most celebrated wine families, she has created an opportunity to pass on a vast amount of vital information about winemaking at the highest level, but also about wine appreciation: in her lucid accounts of tasting she clearly relishes the wines themselves. These are intimate and privileged accounts of people Fiona properly sees as her peers, studied at leisure by a gifted writer, matched with a photographer able to capture countless telling details. Reading *10 Great Wine Families* is the nearest anyone will get to unhurried and uninhibited visits to some of the world's most precious wine properties.

Contents

SUMMER

Familia Torres – Penedès, Spain
Regeneration in Catalonia
p12

Marchesi de' Frescobaldi – Tuscany, Italy
Wine saves a medieval dynasty
p38

Weingut Emmerich Knoll – Wachau, Austria
A phoenix rising beside the Danube
p66

AUTUMN

Famille Thienpont – Bordeaux, France
Belgium colonizes the Right Bank of Bordeaux
p94

Descendientes de J Palacios – Bierzo, Rioja, Priorat, Spain
Pilgrims, pioneers and matadors
p126

Niepoort Ports & Wines – Douro Valley, Portugal
A varietal uprising in the Douro
p154

WINTER

Gaja – Barbaresco, Italy
Maestros and earth goddesses
p184

Egon Müller – Scharzhofberg, Mosel, Germany
Man, mountain, river and grape
p214

SPRING

Liger-Belair – Burgundy, France
Restoring a *grand cru* heritage
p242

Famille Perrin – Rhône, France
Family collaboration
p268

Conclusion p292

SUMMER

Familia Torres
Penedès, Spain

It is hot and sultry in Catalonia as the first grape bunches begin to ripen and the potential of a new harvest is being discovered. I spend time with Miguel Torres Sr and his talented children Miguel Jr and Mireia to find out how a family world famous for its wines is meeting the challenges of the 21st century, especially climate change, and passing the baton from the fourth to the fifth generation.

Marchesi de' Frescobaldi
Tuscany, Italy

A noble Florentine family tracing its roots back to medieval times has been saved thanks to its successful and dynamic wine business. My journey with Lamberto Frescobaldi, the current president and member of the 30th generation of the family, takes us through its history, wines and castles in Tuscany as the grapes approach ripeness in the heat of summer.

Weingut Emmerich Knoll
Wachau, Austria

Thirty years ago, the death knell was tolled for the fledgling Austrian wine industry dealt due to a wine scandal. Today, these wines are the darlings of the world's best wine lists. The Knoll family based in the tiny village of Unterloiben, alongside the Danube, is revered above others for the purity and elegance of its wines. Meeting Emmerich Knoll as harvest approaches provided an incredible insight into the great potential of Austria.

Gateway to the Torres estate

Familia Torres

Regeneration in Catalonia

The story of Torres is a wonderful way to start a book on European wine families. If there is one family that has been able to ensure its survival as well as its impressive success over the last five generations, it is the Torres family. What is remarkable is its fabulous ability to adapt to the trends and talents around it, and as I sit today, tasting a selection of wines made from ancestral grape varieties that I have never heard of before, I marvel at the Torres' inventiveness and resilience. After all, this is the family that shot to global stardom 40 years ago when it pioneered the use of international grapes, especially Chardonnay and Cabernet Sauvignon, in Spain.

It is early summer and the vines have just sprung into life, offering up their buds to the fine weather. As I arrive at Torres, the buds, which look like tiny bunches of grapes, are discernible among the lime green vine leaves, and in a couple of weeks the flowers will appear, ready to be fertilized so that another vine cycle can begin. Here in Penedès, in the heart of Catalonia, there is energy, innovation and promise.

Conquering the world from Catalonia

But perhaps I should start with a bit of history. Although with the current political situation the Torres family does not want to be drawn into the Catalonian Question, it certainly possesses the Catalonian qualities of hard work, discipline and punctuality. While most people think of Catalonia as the home of Cava, Spain's most famous if not so glorious sparkling wine, the still wine market has been dominated by Torres for the last 50 years.

Catalonia has always been an independent, mercantile power. Trade from its ports across the Mediterranean was one of the keys to its success and wealth. Straddling the border between France and Spain in the northeast corner of the country, the region was invaded by Greeks, Romans and Moors until it formed an alliance with Charlemagne, hoping for its independence. Its hopes were dashed when Barcelona was incorporated into the Frankish Empire until the betrothal of Count Berenguer of Barcelona and Petronella, the daughter of the King of Aragon, merged the two regions in 1137 and a golden age began. Catalonia stretched at one time from Languedoc in the north to Valencia in the south and comprised the valuable islands of Corsica, Sardinia, Sicily and Naples as well as parts of Greece and Turkey. Wine was among the valuable goods traded.

After the marriage of Ferdinand of Aragon to Isabella of Castile in 1469, Catalonia lost out as authority and influence moved westwards with the royal court. For the next few centuries, it was buffeted between ruling powers, each promising the region independence if it allied with one power against another. Finally, just before the Spanish Civil War broke out, Catalonia gained autonomous status in 1932. During the Franco years that followed, Catalonia suffered greatly, losing its autonomy, its language and many of its trading privileges.

By the time autonomy was reintroduced in 1978, Catalonia was a broken region. Yet fast-forward to today and it is again a territory bubbling with industry, technology and innovation; its capital, Barcelona, has become a major cultural and gastronomic centre, offering the glories of Gaudí and Dalí alongside those of Ferran Adrià and the Roca brothers. It has become such a prized tourist destination that the city is looking into ways to limit the flow of visitors each year.

The old Renault used by Grandfather Miguel to sell his wines around Europe

The Mas La Plana winery in Pacs, central Penedès, the heart of Bodegas Torres

Torres had been growing grapes in Catalonia since the 17th century but the winery as we know it today was founded in 1870. The family first acted as *négociants* and its small wine museum is full of fascinating bottles from the beginning of the 20th century; its famous Coronas brand name, for example, was registered in 1907. The bodegas were situated right next to the railway line in Vilafranca (as the name implies, the town had tax free status), strategically placed so that the barrels could be rolled out of the cellar and straight onto the train bound for Barcelona.

The winery had been bombed in 1939 as part of collateral damage inflicted by the Civil War and so Miguel Torres realized that if he wanted to survive in the wine business during the troubled years (Civil War followed by World War II and Franco's regime), he would have to look for markets outside Europe. He set off for the Americas where he established excellent contacts in Mexico, the United States, Canada and Cuba. A telegram he sent from Havana to the family in 1942 reads: 'First important order guaranteed. Activate works reconstruction winery – Miguel Torres.'

While Miguel was conquering the Americas, his son studied chemistry in Barcelona and oenology in Dijon, graduating in the early 1960s. Father and son were to work side by side for several decades, just as Miguel Junior does today with his children. In the family museum is the old taupe-coloured Renault in which father Miguel used to travel around Europe selling the Sangre de Toro wine he'd launched in 1954 wherever he could. When he died in 1991, he had spent 59 years building up the company.

If his father was a pioneer in conquering new markets, the younger Miguel (now Miguel Senior) was good at thinking outside the box. He wanted to have more control of the winemaking, insisting on stainless steel tanks and temperature control. He also wanted to control yields and improve quality by planting his vineyards with higher vine density. Thirdly, he aspired to jump onto the international bandwagon by planting Cabernet Sauvignon and Chardonnay grapes. He became famous within the wine world in 1979 when his Cabernet-dominated Gran Coronas Black Label 1970 (now called Mas La Plana) beat many of the most famous names in Bordeaux at a blind tasting organized by *Gault Millau* magazine. It is easy to underestimate the significance of that result today. Forty years ago, the standard-bearers of fine wine were found in Bordeaux; any aspiring producer or region had to take on its 'Classed Growths' if they wanted the world to sit up and take notice. For Torres, sit up they certainly did.

To begin, with the grapes for Torres' wines came from vineyards at Pacs del Penedès which surrounded the winery, the museum and the house of Miguel Torres Sr. After the war years, Barcelona's mayor encouraged winemakers to produce decent red wines by offering valuable subsidies and incentives. Penedès was the biggest wine producing region near Barcelona and it had one huge advantage: it generates variety. From the warm, loamy soils of the coast to the cool, high altitude vineyards inland, Penedès proved it could grow just about any grape variety, from Xarel-lo and Macabeo grapes for the sparkling Cava wines to Tempranillo and Cabernet for the long-lived red wines.

Then later, in order to meet the growing demand for easy drinking, good value wines, the Torres family encouraged the rather generic appellation of Catalunya (Catalonia), appreciating the flexibility it still gives them today to blend across so many different climates and regions for its everyday wines. Torres buys grapes from many different growers, but it never buys wine, preferring the quality control it can exert in making its own wines. Although the family might cringe at the thought, I, like many, remember tasting my first Torres wine: it was an easy drinking red wine in a burgundy shaped bottle with a little plastic black bull dangling from the capsule, served at a student party. It was Sangre de Toro ('bull's blood'), the first really successful Spanish brand worldwide.

Since then, a lot of innovation and experimentation has taken place with the Catalunya appellation being used for a large variety of wines. The family has looked to the more exciting (geologically speaking) areas of Conca de Barberà north of Tarragona and to regions such as Priorat, Ribera del Duero, Rueda, Rías Baixas and Rioja in order to produce increasingly high quality, 'terroir'-driven wines. (Terroir is a French word, often used in the wine business, for which there is really no exact translation. It refers to the five factors – the soil, exposure to the sun, water availability, climate and the work of man – that culminate in a wine which has an exact sense of place.)

Today, Torres makes over 60 different wines from 10 different regions; owns more than 2,000 hectares of vines of which 800 are organic; grows 25 different grape varieties (not including the 'ancestrals' which you will read about a little farther on), and produces 31 different brands, all of which are under the guardianship of Miguel's children Mireia and Miguel Junior. I have trouble keeping up with all the different wines Torres produces as well as its different wineries such as Jean Leon, not to mention the projects in Chile, China and California.

Miguel Torres first planted six hectares of Cabernet Sauvignon in Penedès between 1965 and 1966. The famous Gran Coronas Black Label was, with the 1970 vintage, the first wine to benefit from this grape, in a blend of 70% Cabernet Sauvignon, 20% Tempranillo and 10% Monastrell. Since the 1978 vintage, Gran Coronas Reserva has been made primarily from Cabernet Sauvignon grapes. In 1995, having shown what it was capable of, the Cabernet Sauvignon became a single varietal wine grown in a single, now 29-hectare site called Mas La Plana that surrounds the home of Miguel Torres. When some parcels of Mas La Plana are not up to scratch, they can be declassified into the Gran Coronas Reserva blend.

These vineyards are not very spectacular to look at: they are composed of layers of gravel, sand and clay, a dusty yellow-grey-brown in colour. They remind me of the soils found in Napa Valley in California and I realize that there are comparisons between the two regions. When American pioneer Robert Mondavi established his winery at the end of the 1960s, he planted all his different grape varieties on the valley floor; Europeans visiting at that time were astonished to see Cabernet (a Bordeaux grape) growing next to Chardonnay (a Burgundy grape) when, back home, these varieties demanded completely different soils and climates. It worked, as there was ample sunshine and water on hand. Yet with time and experience, both Mondavi and Torres understood that, for further complexity, they would need to head for the hills.

Ancestral varieties

Penedès is typical Mediterranean country. Along the coast, sandy beaches and coves welcome hordes of holidaymakers in the summer, while inland, small medieval villages reached by winding roads reveal the remnants of old monasteries and castles nestled into the scrubland and pine forests. More and more, this has become superb cycling terrain and I have been greeted a couple of times recently by packs of Lycra-clad bottoms as I swing around a corner. Topping off the Penedès like a tiara are the impressive Montserrat Mountains. Sculpted by millennia of wind and rain, these limestone rocks trap several different microclimates, from hot and windy to mild and damp. Sea winds can blow in maritime fog and rain, providing enough moisture for growing grapes.

Miguel Torres has used his vineyards for much experimentation. He has defied local traditions by planting with more density so that the vines' roots had to compete with each other for nutrients and water. This helped to control plant vigour, as a vine, if not tamed and trellised, can grow incredibly fast and wild. Miguel also believes that 'the more we care for the earth, the better our wine', and this has become a leitmotif that governs much of the viticulture today. With thousands of hectares of vines, Torres is a force to be reckoned with.

So, to return to my fascinating tasting at the Torres bodega. Lined up in front of me is a series of numbered glasses. It represents one of the most exciting Torres projects, and I believe shows the greatness of this family. It is one of the key reasons why Torres has been chosen to open this book on wine families.

Around 30 years ago, Miguel Torres started to plant old Catalan grape varieties that many felt had become extinct after the devastating plague of phylloxera that hit Europe in the late 19th century. This was a mass infestation of little insects that ate through vine roots, leading to the destruction of most of Europe's vineyards. The phylloxera epidemic was only stopped when the vines were grafted onto resistant American rootstocks; so, today, almost all of the famous wines in the world are made from vines with American roots.

Miguel's son and daughter, Miguel Jr and Mireia, took on the project and around 50 Catalan varieties were rediscovered; six of which have proved to be extremely interesting for wine purposes. Placing advertisements in local newspapers, Miguel Torres Jr asked farmers to get in touch if they came across vines that they did not recognize. The first variety to be identified was called Garro. It took 10 years checking for diseases and viruses, cleaning the plant material and then propagating it in vitro, studying its potential to adapt and to produce interesting wines until, having passed all the tests, Garro was planted in the Conca de Barberà region and added to the blend of the first

The new Waltraud winery, named after Miguel Torres Sr's wife

Grans Muralles vintage in 1996. Two years later, the Querol variety, named after the village where Garro was found, followed. The project has been so successful that the plan is to expand it to other Spanish regions such as Rioja, Ribera de Duero and Rías Baixas.

Miguel Jr speaks with enthusiasm: 'It is lovely to be out in nature; to go and check on the vines in the spring up in the Fransola vineyard in the Costers del Segre. We are at 900 metres altitude up there and it is just beautiful.' Such beauty translates into the glass as I try a white wine called Forcada, named after a hill that has the shape of two prongs of a fork (*forcada* means fork in Catalan). It is planted in clay soils at the highest point of Penedès, at 450 metres, and has quite high acidity due to a long growing cycle.

As I taste the 2015, the nose of oatmeal, honey, almonds and citrus fruits and the fresh balance blow me away. Next to it, the 2016 is cooler and steelier and the 2017 is sweeter with a floral, almond paste flavour. I am delighted to be tasting a new grape and months afterwards I still believe that this is one of the most exciting wines I have tasted all year. It is tempting to describe the other wines that I loved among the ancestral varieties, including Gonfaus and Moneu, but I have so much else to tell you about the Torres family that I cannot allow myself to be sidetracked so early into this book. I will just say that, although I don't think that these grapes will become household names, I do hope one day you get a chance to taste them.

Torres & Earth

I spend a day visiting the Torres campus in Pacs del Penedès. There are signs of the vast commercial operation that is the beating heart of the company. Today, there are 1,300 employees around the world, of which at least 300 are based in China. We start at the old historic cellars opposite the modernized office building. We bump into Miguel Sr beaming and tanned, just returned from a trip to Cuba. Torres has been selling wines there for a very long time but there is a slight problem with the government not paying its wine bills. Miguel's mission was to politely remind the powers that be that a one-year delay was not acceptable. 'It's okay now,' he tells me smiling. 'Cuba is doing great now that tourism has opened up the country. Do you know that last year they had five million tourists visiting?'

Next stop is an information pavilion that illustrates the research that Torres is doing into climate change; the topic that is probably the most discussed and debated in the wine world at the moment, although Miguel Sr says: 'What we do never seems to get the public's attention; people seem to ignore information that is not comfortable.' I meet Miquel Rosell-Fieschi, an oceanographer and scientist on Torres' climate change team. Every year 11% of the company profits are invested in environment and climate change related projects, from renewable energy to a biomass boiler; to date over €12 million has been invested. Rosell-Fieschi explains some of his research into the possibility of producing methane to power machinery and reusing carbon dioxide (produced during grape fermentation) to create solvents for other industries.

It was Al Gore's 2006 film *An Inconvenient Truth* that rang alarm bells with Torres. The company has pledged to reduce carbon emissions between 2008 and 2020 by 30% per bottle. In 2017 it had reached a level of 25% in comparison with 2008. Torres believes that temperature increases of more than 2°C could have catastrophic consequences for the wine industry and the only way to combat this is to reduce the amount of carbon dioxide (CO_2) in the atmosphere by reducing carbon emissions. Miguel Sr insists that the wine sector has the capacity to lead the adoption of CO_2 capture and reuse technologies.

This is all part of the Torres & Earth project, the most extensive scheme I have seen in the wine business and one of the achievements for which Miguel Sr will be most remembered. (A large part of the Torres website deals in great detail with the various research initiatives and the partnerships it has formed with universities and energy companies.) Thanks to his efforts (I have heard him speak about climate change on many occasions in the last year), word *is* getting out, and as I explain later in the book, the top wine producers are now addressing the challenges of climate change seriously.

We move onto the Waltraud Cellar, the winery opened in 2008 for the top wines. It is named after Miguel Sr's German wife who played a key part in building up the winery, developing the German market, and who has presided over the Miguel Torres Foundation for many years. Gleaming stainless steel, state of the art sorting machines, rows of French oak barrels and gravity transfer equipment encased in very quiet and sober surroundings all have the slightly unfortunate effect of enforcing the technical over the human aspect of wines.

Family ties

At lunch we sit down with the two Miguels and Mireia. It has taken a Herculean effort by the PR Director to get this to happen and the lunch is rather a rushed and somewhat tense affair held in the family restaurant that is heavy on plastic and prints and a little past its sell-by date. Miguel Sr keeps

Miguel Torres Jr, Miguel Torres Sr, and Mireia Torres transfer power between the generations

restaurant in Hollywood and friend to the stars. As you enter the winery, all is glamour, curves, colour and fun. The décor is jazz-like cool, music plays over the speakers, comfortable sofas and tasting bars adorn the visitors' centre; the founder's name is written in neon in the cellar; the labels hark back to the 1950s; and the wines are named after key facts of Jean Leon's life.

As we walk around, I can see Mireia becoming more animated, more liberated as she tells me: 'Here, I can do what I want.' She naturally has a quiet, rather studious air but here I see her blue eyes light up behind her glasses, as her precise mouth breaks into a big smile and her charm shines through. The wines are decent and democratically priced, and Mireia admits that they are consciously targeting millennials with them. But just before I might think that everything at Jean Leon is about art and culture, glamour and marketing, Mireia tells me about a drip irrigation project she has here and how a water diviner managed to find a valuable source 300 metres down. 'The only problem was that he was going to charge me €40,000 to drill the hole,' she laughs. 'But hey, there is more to life than scientific knowledge, so I agreed. We found a source with the potential of 10,000 litres of water per hour. Now with drip irrigation we can manage the vineyard better.'

Beyond Penedès

The next morning, I embark with Miguel Jr for Priorat where Torres was making wine in the 1920s. As we enter the slip road at Vilafranca, we laugh at the road sign forbidding donkey carts on the motorway; evidently time has not moved that quickly in Penedès. Miguel talks frankly about his life abroad. 'I returned from Chile in 2012; I wanted to stay longer but my father had management problems and I needed to come back to support him. When you return home after being away, you see more beauty. When I was a child I took things here for granted, but now I love what we are doing, the ancestral varieties for example. My father's legacy will be Mas La Plana; I hope ours will be these grapes which are so much part of our heritage.'

As we drive, we talk about Catalan politics and the recent attempt at independence. It has led several big companies, including CaixaBank and

Codorníu, to move their headquarters to other regions in Spain. 'We make wine, not politics,' Miguel answers and cites how wine can unite people: one Torres wine, Milmanda, was served at the dinner that brought Presidents Castro and Obama together.

Our first stop is Porrera; at 550 metres it is one of the freshest zones in Priorat. We are near the Serra de Prades mountain range, which runs east to west forming rocky outcrops and cliffs where eagles circle, winds blow in from the north and the holm oaks, chestnuts, firs and gorse bend towards the sea. This is wild country, abandoned for many years for being too harsh and difficult to farm, but now it is considered as probably the most exciting viticultural zone in Spain. Rather by accident, Priorat will appear twice in this book as each of the two great Spanish families I have chosen have been drawn to this haunting region. I am sure that both Miguel Torres and Alvaro Palacios have different methods and philosophies about the wines they produce here. Their wineries are in sight of each other, less than five kilometres apart, and yet in the wine business there is room for many different interpretations; this is one of its most magical elements.

As we walk through the vineyards, Miguel tells me what he loves about Priorat. Here, the focus is on the Garnacha and Cariñena grapes (which over the French border are known as Grenache and Carignan). He especially likes Cariñena, which he feels expresses the soil differences better, and there is a lot of old vine Cariñena in the region. Our next stop is Santuari de la Rosa, a beautiful amphitheatre of a vineyard nestled under the shadow of mountains. This is an enchanting place that buzzes with life and promise, the old vines offering up their fresh green shoots and leaves to the sun as their vegetative cycle begins again. For Miguel it is one of the best sites in Priorat, a 2.5-hectare parcel with old bush vines that are more than 70 years old. The soils of Priorat are a mixture of slate and schist with high acidity and the ability to withstand droughts. I wonder whether Santuari de la Rosa will one day be made as a single vineyard wine or be blended into the two Torres Priorat wines: the flagship wine Perpetual, and Salmos.

Perpetual is made from vines that are between 80 and 100 years old, the fruit either grown by Torres or purchased from local wine growers. Perpetual is dark and intense, rich with dark fruit flavours and dense with ripe

The great hall at Rèmole with the Albizi crest

of small rooms where I spend a fascinating morning trawling through the family's papers. These works were gathered together by Lisa Frescobaldi, widow of Dino, Lamberto's uncle who was a celebrated journalist for Rome's *Corriere della Sera* newspaper and author of the Frescobaldi family history. I am flabbergasted by the somewhat casual manner in which I am introduced to this treasure trove. Apart from donning gloves, there is little ceremony as I travel through the centuries, keenly aware of the privilege that I have been granted as the first non-academic to have access to these documents. Going through the archives, I manage to find more pieces of the family jigsaw.

There have been a few dips in the family's fortunes. Around the end of the 16th century the Frescobaldi went bankrupt, buried under a pile of bad debts (some of them from Henry VIII, others from unpaid loans to Pope Leo X). The letters and the great regal seals of Henry VIII are amazing to behold and I love the fact that they are here, tangible, living, accessible. As a result of a century-long struggle against the rival Medici family (at that time at the height of its powers), the Frescobaldi were banished from Florence and excluded from any positions of power. Only in the 17th century could they return to the centre of the city's social and political life. To celebrate this event, Matteo Frescobaldi commissioned Lorenzo Lippi to paint posthumous portraits of his illustrious ancestors.

Today, these Lippi portraits have been assembled at Rèmole and offer an impressive showcase of the Frescobaldi family at the height of its power. In the great hall the portraits are offset by large tapestries emblazoned with the Albizi crest, for it was this family that saved the fortunes of the Frescobaldi by bringing the wealthy estates of Rèmole, Pomino and Nipozzano to the family in the 19th century through marriage. Rèmole is also the site of the chapel where members of the Frescobaldi family are buried. It is a sober, quiet place, belying the tumultuous lives of those who slumber here.

The couple who were responsible for saving the Frescobaldi dynasty, Leonia Albizi and Angiolo Frescobaldi, who were married in 1863. Angiolo, the last surviving heir of the Frescobaldi at that time, was a very cultivated man, an avid art collector who set about restoring and buying back on the open market any family portraits that he could find. Fortunately, the couple had a son, Ferdinando, who assured the future of the Frescobaldi lineage.

The newly acquired Tenuta Perano in Chianti Classico

the world are always political.' Gaiole is one of the historical little villages of Chianti that are surrounded by beautiful wineries. Famous names such as Ricasoli and Castello di Ama are its neighbours. Graced with an amphitheatre of vineyards and high elevation with chalky, limestone soils, just as with Castelgiocondo in Montalcino, Frescobaldi farmed the land and made the wine since 2014. Then when the estate went bankrupt in 2017, the company bought it.

The first vintage, 2014, was sold off in bulk but the 2015, which has just been released for sale, is beautifully balanced between fruit and oak with a great freshness and a pinch of savoury bitterness. Picking up the bottle, I notice its simple label with the Frescobaldi crest: it shows the goddess of Destiny with a veil-like banner bearing the family motto *Spera in Deo* (We believe in God). The veil is billowing out like a sail behind her, filled by the winds of commerce that have served the family so well for over eight centuries. Lamberto tells me that in the 12th century, Tuscany was still somewhat pagan and so to declare your Christian belief was quite a statement.

On my last evening in Florence, I dine with Lamberto, Eleanora, their son Carlo and Alexandre James the photographer at the Frescobaldi restaurant in the Piazza Signoria, opposite the Uffizi Gallery. It is crowded and lively and we can eat outside on the large terrace with delicious Tuscan classics and, of course, a wide array of Frescobaldi wines. Over dinner I rather casually ask Lamberto if there are other projects that I should know about and he spends quite some time talking to me about Laudemio, the family olive oil; about how tourism has become so important that each of the estates has guest rooms and catering facilities; about the expansion of the Frescobaldi wine bars and restaurants and how they only use Tuscan products.

The Frescobaldi may no longer count themselves among the great bankers or political powerbrokers of today, but over the last 50 years they have built up a very impressive wine empire. Under the aristocratic demeanour beats a more bourgeois, commercial heart. It is this mercantile instinct that accounts for the family's longevity. Future generations of the family will need to earn their spurs in the company, firstly by getting a good university education and then by demonstrating that they can also earn their living elsewhere.

During the harvest in 2017, I invited Lamberto's oldest son, Vittorio, to come and work in our wine cellar at Le Pin. He was so excited that he could get his boots on and help us with the pumping over of the vats during fermentation. 'This is great,' he exclaimed: 'I never get to do this at home.' Evidently another generation of Frescobaldi is waiting in the wings.

Lamberto's three children, Vittorio, Leonia and Carlo, as well as most of his nephews, are all preparing to take the reins. It is safe to say that the 800-year old heritage is in good hands. Since they were born, the business has gone from strength to strength and now is of the size and scope that it can offer attractive career opportunities for the next bright Frescobaldi generation. There may be challenges in running a family business; it still has to work on the image and recognition of its wines; there may be frailties and faults, but the Frescobaldi are a tightly knit clan who for the most part admire the work of their president. As I take leave of Lamberto at the airport, his final words are echoes of what he has previously told me: 'I need more wine; I need more time.'

Fiona's favourite Frescobaldi wines

Lamaione from Castelgiocondo

Lamaione is made from 100% Merlot grapes. It has sweet berry flavours on the palate – mulberries and cherries – followed by warmer, more complex notes of chocolate, almond, coffee and mint. Aged for two years in oak barrels, it is powerfully expressive with densely packed tannins. This wine is usually drunk far too young and could do with at least 10–20 years cellaring before being enjoyed.

Montesodi from Nipozzano

It would be remiss not to include a wine made from 100% Sangiovese grapes – Tuscany's greatest native variety. Produced solely from a single vineyard at an elevation of 400 metres only in exceptional years, Montesodi has great length and elegance. It has the classic aromas of cherry liqueur, violets and blueberries that give way to more complex notes of ginger, wood smoke and almonds. Great ageing potential.

Giramonte from Castiglioni

A recent discovery for me is the velvety texture and smooth blend of Merlot and Sangiovese grapes. Aged in French oak barrels, this is typical of the Frescobaldi winemaking style: lots of warm, fruit-forward flavours, aromas of damson plums, wild cherries and blackberries, sweet and fresh on the palate with a firm finish and round tannins.

Ferro from Collazzi

I have to admit an interest here because I first pointed out to Lamberto Frescobaldi that his Petit Verdot grapes at Collazzi would make a great single varietal wine. Produced from 100% Petit Verdot and only made in top years, it is firm and fresh on the nose with lively fruit flavours of redcurrants and wild strawberries. This wine has great structure and presence in the mouth with good chocolate flavoured tannins and excellent oak integration.

Leonia from Pomino

A sparkling wine made to honour Leonia Frescobaldi who in the 19th century planted French grape varieties at Pomino and won a gold medal at the World's Fair in Paris in 1878. Rich, full and expressive on the nose, its ripe orchard fruity notes give way to honey and brioche flavours. This wine's purity of expression and round, full mouthfeel is most impressive – one of the best sparkling Italian wines that I have ever tasted.

Views over the Danube and vineyards from the Pfaffenberg to the Kellerberg

Weingut Emmerich Knoll

A phoenix rising beside the Danube

Austrian wines are hot. They are found on the wine lists of the world's best restaurants, and today the top producers are spoken about with the same awe as those of Burgundy and Bordeaux. That this small land-locked country has arrived at this level of wine fame is something of a miracle, especially when you consider all the hurdles it has had to overcome.

I have travelled to the Wachau on the northern shore of the River Danube to meet the Knoll family, one of the finest wine producers in the country with a wonderful story that exemplifies part of what makes wine families great: a sense of identity, a history grounded in a region and a wine culture that rolls along with the passing years, evolving without losing sight of its roots. Weingut Knoll produces wines from the local Grüner Veltliner and Riesling grapes. With these two white varieties it makes about 25 bottlings from different vineyard sites harvested at various levels of ripeness, offering up a vivid lesson in Austrian *terroir*, history and winemaking.

As I get out of the car, the dry heat hits me after many kilometres of air-conditioning. There is a stillness in the air, a suspension as if everyone has deserted their posts for the August holidays. The tarmac bubbles slightly and sticks to my shoes; a mirage glistens in the distance. Through its middle, an elderly man strides towards me – surprisingly sure-footed. As he reaches me, I stop him and in my meagre words of German confirm my location: 'Gross', 'Leibenhof' and 'Gelb', he nods. I step back in the car muttering my '*Vielen dank*' and vowing to learn German when I have some free time.

What then follows is a sort of Tom and Jerry farce where I am ringing the doorbell of the modern Weingut Knoll while Alexandre James, the photographer, is also at the door of the Weingut Knoll but he is at the old, picturesque winery just in front on the parallel street. Our host, Emmerich Knoll, strides backwards and forwards between both doors, keen to corral us both before we upset the calm and stability that reign in the peaceful hamlet of Unterloiben.

Between river and hillside

Everywhere there is tranquility. We stand on a small village road sandwiched between the rather murky beige and silver waters of the mighty Danube and the verdant steep slopes of vineyards rising up to the mountains. Luckily Emmerich's English is good and he smiles benignly down at us from his impressive height. Calm is restored and out of nowhere, Herr Knoll Senior appears magically, as he will do throughout our stay. Is he lurking in the background or does he have a telepathic link to his eldest son? Elegant and proud with a straight gait, a firm jawline, lush silver hair and clear blue eyes, it is clear that Emmerich Sr is still very much a presence to be reckoned with in this family. 'He is interested in so many things,' the younger Emmerich tells us with admiration, 'music, opera, history'. However much the father may say that his son is now in charge, Emmerich Junior says simply that no official transition has taken place yet and the paterfamilias is still a formidable authority.

Walking through a vineyard is a great icebreaker. Talking nature, talking viticulture, looking at wild flowers that carpet the vine rows, watching the cabbage whites flit among the vine leaves, hearing the buzz of insects and the

and stand the trials of weather and time; in 2002, terrible rains led to thousands of square metres of wall being damaged. The stones store warmth and release it during the nights; their mortar-free structure allows water and rainfall to flow easily through their barriers, and they form a natural habitat for all sorts of insects and wild animals that each play their part in the fauna of the vineyards.

The Knoll heritage is out here on these slopes and the family look after it carefully. When a vineyard parcel needs to be replanted, cuttings are taken from the best-looking vines. The estate comprises 18 hectares, divided up into 70 different parcels over six different vineyard sites, each made up of slate, granite or loess, sandy alluvial soils. They include famous names such as Schütt, Loibenberg, Kellerberg and Kreutles in the Wachau and a small part of the Pfaffenberg vineyard in Kremstal. You may not be familiar with these designations but as you get to know Knoll's wines, you recognize them on the labels and begin to understand their individual characteristics.

Above the town of Dürnstein, for example, lies the famous Kellerberg vineyard, situated on gneiss rock (a kind of metamorphic igneous granite) and facing south and east as it rounds the bend of the river. Cool air flowing down through the gullies makes for wines that are tauter and have more acidity than those from Loibenberg. Loibenberg is the biggest of the vineyard sites and its hillside terraces with dark, rich soils are situated behind the Knoll winery; it is the most famous site of the eastern Wachau, dating from 1861, a 25-hectare hillside that is much warmer than Kellerberg, even if the steep slopes that drop 200 metres vertically down to the village mitigate the heat. Today, no matter where you are in the world, the idea of *crus* or individual parcels has become increasingly important as wine growers begin to understand their soils better.

Each vineyard has its own topography: Pfaffenberg – which takes its name from an old slang word for a priest – is shallow and dry, an ancient riverbed 80 metres above the Danube where only Riesling, which can handle dry soils, grows. Grüner Veltliner needs richer earth and is therefore found at the foot of the hills or on the valley floor. All vineyard work is done by hand (even the mini tractors that buzz around the small country lanes cannot be used on the terraces) and the Knolls need about 1,200 to 1,500 hours of labour per year compared to the 50 to 200 hours needed to work vineyards on the flat.

It is a common mistake to believe that valley vineyards are not as good as terraces because they are less well drained. In fact, one of the most exciting Knoll sites is Schütt, both for Riesling and Grüner Veltliner, formed eons ago by a torrent roaring down the mountain and fanning out into an alluvial basin. It is a cool site because fresh air is driven down from the mountain gully; it has stony, gneissy, sandy soil and the wines always have fresh acidity in them.

I dwell on these vineyard sites because one of the magic qualities of the Knoll wines is that you taste their different characteristics in the wine. Pfaffenberg is warm and ripe; Schütt is fresh and yet powerful; Kellerberg is fresh, precise and racy. As Emmerich says: 'We know the personality of our vineyards really well.'

In the morning a gentle westerly wind tends to brush over the area but on the hot late August days when I visited, there is no breeze and it is wonderful to find respite in the cellars. We cross the road to Emmerich's parents' house which is really just an extension of the cellar. Stepping inside is like walking into a painting by Vermeer: there are ancient tiles on the floor, heavy oak chiselled furniture, a faded piece of tapestry decorates a table, a clock sounding out a centuries-old reassuring tick tock on the dresser. A heavy wooden door leads to the press room that for years has welcomed the grapes into the winery. Custom-made pails are stacked up in the corner ready for the next harvest.

The village harvest starts on the flat of the valley floor with Traminer at the beginning of September, and continues until the end of October. At Knoll, a simple quality selection is made in the vineyard before the grapes arrive: one stick in the trailer full of grapes going back to the winery denotes top quality, two sticks second quality and so on. The grapes are macerated in utilitarian vats at cool temperatures for up to one day before crushing, and unusually, after pressing, the press wine is combined immediately with the free run juice. This contributes enormously to the Knoll wine style: these wines are not as crisp and fruity as others but they have more backbone, more character and more longevity; their pure intensity builds over the years.

Then we descend to the cellar; dimly lit, it takes a while for my eyes to get used to the gloom. Large oval shadows gleam polished and sacred as rich surfaces emerge from the dark. I run my hand over the front of an old wooden vat; it is gnarled and bobbled. I look closer. It is magnificently carved in an old gothic script with the name of Emmerich and his date of birth, 21st of March

The Knoll family: Anya, Emmerich and Baby Emmerich the 4th

which serves up delicious traditional local dishes accompanied exclusively by the Knoll family wines. Sitting under the dappled fading light glittering through the late summer apple trees – their branches already sagging under the weight of the fruit – I am reminded of the Seurat painting of *A Sunday on La Grande Jatte*, as the waitresses in their traditional Austrian folk dresses glide among the tables in a timeless tableau. Here again at the end of a long day, I feel enveloped by the warmth and stability of the region as we sip a 2013 Kellerberg Riesling with fresh notes of green apple, pear, mineral stoniness and a dry, abiding purity.

The next morning I am woken by the church bells and descend to see the house in full action. Yoda the black retriever languidly thumps his tail as I pass; swallows flit and dive among the roof eves; Emmerich's mother Monika, in traditional Austrian dress, darts bird-like among the rooms, a duster in her hands. She is often found working in the vineyards at this hour. Julian, Anja and Emmerich's son, resplendent in his football kit, helps feed his cherubic brother, Baby Emmerich, in the kitchen.

Emmerich Sr suggests that he takes us on a tour of Dürnstein to show us the baroque splendour of the monastery with its blue belfry that looks out over the Danube and the ruins of the ancient medieval castle perched high up on the hill. We hike up to the top of the castle. Mountain goat like, Emmerich Sr strides nimbly up the hill, leaving us trailing in his wake. Far below us, the Danube flows slowly and sedately through the Wachau bend. On the other bank of the river the ancient Göttweig Abbey stands sentinel over these hallowed vineyards. When it is really hot, Emmerich Jr swims with his dog from one side of the Danube to the other. I hope he keeps a lookout for the tourist boats!

Emmerich Sr is quite a Renaissance man, much to the admiration of his son. At the top of the new house he has built himself a private art gallery celebrating a local painter, Siegfried Stoitzner from Dürnstein. Working at the beginning of the 20th century, it was Stoitzner who painted the statue of Saint Urban for the Knoll label. His works show an idyllic country life of rural villages, ruddy-faced peasants, angelic children and impressive ruins. 'What happened during the World War II to all of these people?' I ask. Grandmother Johanna, in her 70s, was left to defend the family home from the Russians who occupied this part of Austria as her husband and son were away fighting in the army. She prevented the Russians from shooting holes in the beautiful old vats to get the wine out and was allowed to use French prisoners of war to help her in the vineyards. She insisted that the POWs eat at her table, paid them wages and allowed them to live in the house. After the war, when Europe was on its knees, several of the French men came back of their own free will to work at the estate.

Wachau wines

I have been here for a day and still I haven't sat down to formally taste the wines. Perhaps that is part of the magic; the fact that to really appreciate them, you first need to learn about their roots. I have to declare at this stage that I am a Riesling nut. I adore this grape variety, the sheer, compelling purity and refreshingly juicy fruit; the crunchiness of the wine as it swirls around my palate; the myriad of flavours that are thrown up like a kaleidoscope; and the perfect pitch of balance between freshness and richness, between sweet aroma and bone dry finish. While I respect Grüner Veltliner and its uniquely Austrian heritage, I find the wines fuller bodied, more peach and melon in their aromas, a touch waxy, richer and more generous with just enough acidity to balance them.

Emmerich Jr is President of the Wachau wine growers' association called Vinea Wachau, which was founded in 1983, groundbreakingly early. In the beginning there were only 24 members; today, there are 200 representing 95% of the vineyards – including 124 recognized single vineyard sites – from internationally known producers to small crop holders. People help their neighbours; there is a democracy of vote and expression. 'In order to keep the region alive we needed to join together as growers to protect the Wachau from cheaper grown grapes from neighbouring areas,' Papa Emmerich explains. There is more solidarity in the Wachau as a result than in many other wine growing regions in the world. This is not easy to achieve; like chefs in a restaurant, each wine grower has his own recipe, his own philosophy and is convinced that his way is the best. The lobbying efforts of the Wachau were richly rewarded in 2000 when the region was designated a UNESCO World Heritage Site.

The Wachau even has its own unique wine classification system that includes three categories of wine: Steinfeder, Federspiel and Smaragd. They range in style from fruity, fresh and light, to medium-rich, powerful and full-bodied; each style is determined by the level of ripeness in the grapes and also affects the wine's ability to age. This system has the advantage of being a key selling point for the Wachau while also instilling a sense of unity. This is all well and good, but the trademark names that the Wachau has come up with are just never going to become part of the global wine lexicon. Both Emmerich and August wear little lizard brooches on their lapels when they do tastings; this is the symbol of the Smaragd wines – the glory of the Wachau.

When first instigated in 1984 the Steinfeder category was quite revolutionary. At that time, the style of most wines was adjusted by adding sugar to the grapes before fermentation in a process called chaptalization; it was unheard of to make wines just according to the natural ripeness of the grapes. The new styles also marked a key step in Austria's breaking away from

Fiona's favourite Knoll wines

Grüner Veltliner Schütt

Good intense lemon yellow colour, floral refined aromas with notes of green summer leaves, then jasmine on the nose; a little lighter structure than usual with more minerality than fat, yet with a good tannic backbone and pure pear aromas on the palate; very precise and tight on the finish.

Grüner Veltliner Loibenberg

Charming from the start with warm, creamy aromas of golden plums, white pepper and apple blossom; there is power in the structure and lots of resonance on the palate that leads to a beautiful, generous, warm palate. Ripe and soft, this is very drinkable from the first sip.

Riesling Vinothekfüllung

These wines are made from grapes that have a little botrytis in them (a more welcome type of rot, which shrivels the grapes and makes them sweeter). They are richer than the other grapes and that can hide the specificities of the site. These are wines to cellar and drink several years after they are released. With a fairly hefty alcohol content, the wine has a rich yellow colour, aromas of apricot and mango, fresh acidity, a rich, creamy structure and a juicy, appealing finish.

Riesling Kellerberg

Great intensity with an elegant nose: very fresh scents of linden, summer flowers, a touch of grapefruit peel, elderflower and spice; on the palate the intensity builds up to fill the mouth with structure, freshness and purity; perfect balance between fruit and structure; between alcohol and acidity.

Riesling Schütt

This wine deserves to be drunk with a bit of age, as found with the great 2007 vintage. Bright and shining with a beautiful lemon, gold colour; on the nose there are aromas of petrol, honey, wax, muesli and lots of spice. The palate is round, warm and velvety with exuberant flavours and a touch of botrytis. The last wine I taste while I am at Knoll, its flavours remain with me all the way back to Vienna.

AUTUMN

Famille Thienpont – Bordeaux, France

The Thienponts' Belgian roots are deeply entwined with the history of the Right Bank of Bordeaux and more especially the regions of Pomerol and Saint-Emilion. Three cousins, working closely together, make wines that every wine lover dreams of owning. An intimate portrait of my family from the inside written during harvest time; Jacques Thienpont is my husband.

Descendientes de J Palacios – Bierzo, Rioja, Priorat, Spain

The regeneration of Spanish wines over the last couple of decades has been miraculous due to a few visionaries who have questioned the old way of doing things, pushed out the boundaries of winemaking, renovated abandoned vineyards and identified the best *crus* in the country. Harvest is over, the wines are nestling down in their barrels and I witness the ambition and energy of Alvaro Palacios and his young nephew Ricardo, as we cross the country from west to east, in one intense weekend.

Niepoort Ports & Wines – Douro Valley, Portugal

I arrive in Oporto just as a family drama is exploding; Dirk is pacing up and down, waiting to see whether his sister will accept his offer to buy her out of the century old port company with its Dutch origins. An inside look at the trials that can affect wine estates and an extraordinarily creative winemaker as autumn draws to a close and the vines are shutting down for the winter.

The Thienpont family home at Hof te Cattebeke

Famille Thienpont

Belgium colonizes the Right Bank of Bordeaux

The first time I drove into the courtyard of Hof te Cattebeke in Etikhove, I admit I was a little bit intimidated. This stately manor house in the heart of Flanders, dating back to 1612, has been the home of the Thienpont family for over 400 years. All over the world, there are wine drinkers who know the name 'Etikhove' without ever having setting foot in Belgium. The name echoes through the corridors of Thienpont history and generations of the family make a pilgrimage, even if it's only once in their lifetimes, to visit the family seat.

I have lived at Hof te Cattebeke for over 20 years, longer than I have lived anywhere else in the world. Since my marriage to Jacques Thienpont it has been my home, and so this chapter on the Thienpont family is about my family, and therefore all the more poignant to write. I will try to distance myself, if only by a few paces, from the tale I am about to tell.

The first thing I had to learn when I arrived in Belgium was the family tree (the second was Dutch); it has taken me many years and I have still not mastered all of the second and third cousins, or cousins once or twice removed. Remember that in the years after World War II there was a baby boom and like many good Catholic families in those days with no television, it multiplied. To try to keep things simpler, I have chosen to talk about one winemaker each from three of the main branches. But let's first go back to the family origins.

The Thienponts are a notable Flemish family, living in a small village on the outskirts of Oudenaarde – best-known for its tapestries and for a famous battle that pitted King Louis XIV of France against a British warrior, the Duke of Marlborough, in 1708. The Thienponts have lived quietly here for four centuries, acting as jurists, bailiffs and mayors of the region. During the French Revolution, the house became a haven for fleeing

Wine bottled by Georges Thienpont at Etikhove

priests and aristocrats. In later wars it was to serve as a hospital or as military headquarters. I feel the ghosts of this abundant history in the house often – benign presences that add to the rich fabric of a family and its wines.

In 1842, the family founded a wine merchant business, buying vats of wine from the Douro, Jerez and Bordeaux. One of my favourite places is the underground cellar where ancient barrels can still be found hidden away. In those days it was much easier to transport wine in oak barrels than glass bottles and a wine merchant's reputation was based on his ability to choose the best barrels, and blend and bottle his wine carefully before selling it to the local gentry. The trunk where the family archives are kept stands in the hallway of Hof te Cattebeke and the attics are lined with order books recording many years of clients and transactions. The prices listed would make modern collectors weep. Just occasionally we still find an old bottle with the label of the house, Hof te Cattebeke, and the words 'Bottled by Georges Thienpont – Etikhove'. A few years ago a journalist friend called

Georges Thienpont, formidable grandfather of Jacques, Alexandre and Nicholas

excitedly from a restaurant in New York. At the table next to him, he had spotted a couple of high rollers savouring a bottle of Domaine de la Romanée-Conti Richebourg 1952 bottled at Etikhove.

Etikhove in the Gironde

The Thienpont family is quite a dynasty and the central character is Georges Thienpont, the grandfather of Jacques, Alexandre and Nicolas Thienpont – the three winemakers from three separate branches of the Thienpont clan who today each make celebrated wines. Born and raised at Etikhove, Georges joined the family wine business in 1904 and, like his ancestors, often travelled to Bordeaux to select barrels of wine to sell in Belgium. In 1921, he decided to purchase an estate in Bordeaux that he considered would be a good investment. For years, Bordeaux for Belgians meant the Right Bank, which includes Saint-Emilion, Pomerol and the satellite appellations. Even today, Belgium is the leading market in terms of volume for these wines.

This was because traditionally the Bordeaux wines that the Low Countries purchased were shipped by barge from Libourne through the waterways of France, while the wines of the Médoc sailed to Great Britain, the Hanseatic League and further afield, from the port of Bordeaux. It was only when Napoleon built two bridges at the beginning of the 19th century, one at Libourne and one at Bordeaux over the Dordogne and Garonne rivers, that a suitable link was created from the merchants of Libourne and the wines of the Right Bank to the merchants on the Quai des Chartrons in Bordeaux and the wines of the Médoc.

Scouting around the Libournais, Georges came across an auction for an estate with a magnificent view over the hills to the village of Saint-Emilion. The château he purchased was Troplong Mondot and the vineyards extended over 30 hectares. Three years later he had the opportunity to purchase Vieux Château Certan, one of the few 'real' châteaux in Pomerol, which he took several years to restore to its former glory. A new chapter in the Thienpont Family saga, 'Etikhove in the Gironde', had begun.

View from the cellar door at Le Pin

Jacques Thienpont, creator of Le Pin

Vieux Château Certan, restored to its former glory by the Thienponts

Jacques surveying the Le Pin vines from his office – his trusty bicycle ready should closer inspection be necessary

Le Pin at night

have been fetching on the much-prized Pomerol plateau (today, upwards of €5 million per hectare), many saw the opportunity to cash in. Over the last five years, the number of producers in Pomerol has dropped to under 100. Vieux Château Certan, sitting on the plateau, surrounded by Petrus, L'Evangile and La Conseillante, is one of the largest and includes 14 hectares of vines. The family jokes that the lawn in front of the château must be one of the most expensive in the world as it covers several ares of prime Pomerol *terroir*.

Le Pin and Vieux Château Certan lie close, certain of their respective parcels touching each other. When we are in Pomerol, the whole family takes to bicycles – the distances are just too small to use a car. We love the freedom, the freshness of the air and the opportunity to observe tiny things: a row of daisies in an unploughed patch of vineyard, a new ditch dug to drain the water, freshly formed buds on a south-facing parcel. Thienponts on bicycles are regular sights during harvest time, so do drive carefully in the region! From the original hectare surrounding the winery, Jacques has managed to expand the Le Pin vineyard over the decades to three hectares by buying a few vine rows here and there. Only those parcels that are contiguous to the original estate are used for Le Pin; the rest of the vines are gathered and vinified like Le Pin but blended over three vintages to make a wine called Trilogie, which is sold to private customers and a few close clients.

The story of Le Pin's rise is a little like a fairy tale and Jacques often grins sheepishly when he tells it, as if he still cannot believe his good luck. Jacques looks like a man who is still amazed by his own good fortune. Boyish still in spite of his 70-something years, his broad smile and easy manner surprise those who meet the owner of Le Pin for the first time. He is down to earth and fun, often teasing wine lovers who talk about Le Pin too reverently, generous to all and a father figure for many of the fourth generation of Thienponts who often come to him for advice. He loves wine but he loves his family and his home in Etikhove even more. His pride in and affection for us fills the lives of myself and our two sons, Georges and William. The day after I first met Jacques over 20 years ago, he showed me around the legendary Le Pin. Although I admired the simplicity and the hands-on approach, I must admit to having been quite shocked and a touch dismayed at the rudimentary set-up.

For his first vintages Jacques used a second-hand stainless steel vat for the fermentation and old barrels from Vieux Château Certan for the ageing. When it came to running off the wine after fermentation, usually done from one tank to another, Jacques realized that he had nowhere to put the new wine. He was obliged to put it straight into barrels, thus accidentally starting a trend for the second fermentation (called the malolactic fermentation, it converts tart malic acid to softer lactic acid and stabilizes the wine) to happen in barrels rather than in tanks. This practice is now used at almost every top estate in Bordeaux, especially since it means that the young wine gets put into oak barrels much earlier, making it rounder and softer – ready for the crucial *En Primeur* tastings which happen before the wines are bottled six months later.

As Bordeaux became more of a travel destination, increasing numbers of visitors started to visit Le Pin. Winemaking became more professional; cellars began adapting to increased parcel selection and thus needed more, smaller fermentation vats. Jacques felt the need to build a new winery. But he insisted that the scale should be kept small, in keeping with the vineyard. He called upon Belgian architect Paul Robbrecht to help him. Paul had never designed a cellar before but he understood the need to absorb sound and the importance of angles to throw a play of light throughout the building. In 2011, the new Le Pin winery was inaugurated and Jacques finally had more space to make his wine and an office of his own, looking out over his vines.

The new winery is a smart building made of local stone, with solid oak doors and a slate roof; inside are two rows of small stainless steel conical vats and below that a barrel cellar where the wines are aged for 15 to 18 months. It introduces a new standard of excellence at Le Pin: better hygiene, better temperature control, movement by gravity, and certainly enables more precision in the winemaking and parcel selection. With better knowledge of the soils, wine growers in Bordeaux have begun to divide their vineyards into smaller parcels according to the soil, age of the vine, amount of water retention and exposure to the sun. This has led to each parcel being made and aged separately to fully understand its role in the final blend, hence the need for lots of small fermenting vats.

Harvest time

I ask the photographer, Alexandre James, to meet us in Bordeaux during harvest time. Not only is he guaranteed to find all the Thienponts in town then, but during the vintage, the family members drop in on each other's cellars and share advice and anecdotes about how the picking is going. The closeness of the family is evident. It is an exciting period of the year; as Jacques says: 'We only have one chance to get the vintage right.' Even if we all have many harvests under our belts, everyone will admit to at least a few butterflies in the stomach. As the three cousins, Alexandre, Jacques and Nicolas, exchange vintage tales among themselves, there is a good bit of teasing going on. 'Jacques was born with a rabbit's paw in his hand,' says Nicolas as he witnesses the last beautifully healthy grapes of Le Pin arriving in the cellar.

During my first harvest at Le Pin after my marriage, I was amazed by the simplicity and calm of Jacques' winemaking style. We use the same team of pickers and sorters for both Vieux Château Certan and Le Pin and they will alternate between the two estates depending upon the ripeness of each parcel. Usually dressed in the same shabby sweater and torn jeans, Jacques,

Nicolas' red wines from the Côtes de Francs share a frank expression, a rich, earthy character mixed with scents of plum, cedar, liquorice and pepper. While they have expressive aromas, their texture and body are surprisingly supple. Puygueraud is prized for its rich and spicy flavours and is the most full-bodied of the wines. La Prade is more overtly fruity with a mixture of berry aromas blending well with the oak. The Charmes-Godard red is quite structured and austere when young. The Charmes-Godard Blanc gives Nicolas a chance to vinify a complex white wine that nevertheless has a backbone of freshness and very expressive aromas of white flowers and cream.

In 1994, a new challenge was presented to Nicolas when he was asked to take over the management of Château Pavie Macquin, a Saint-Emilion Grand Cru Classé, beautifully located on the top of the appellation's famed limestone plateau. Since 1986, the estate was farmed according to biodynamic principles. At that time this method of organic farming was new to Bordeaux and the estate suffered several disastrous harvests. Nicolas was delighted to have an opportunity to discover more about this method of organic culture and adopt a more pragmatic approach. The château already had an illustrious

Nicolas Thienpont, the thinker of the family

history in viticulture. It had been purchased in 1897 by Albert Macquin, an agronomic engineer who had successfully developed the revolutionary grafting technique that saved the Bordeaux vines after the phylloxera crisis, where a type of insect imported from America had munched its way through most of the vine roots in Europe. Pavie Macquin is rich and vibrant with very clear, red and black fruit flavours and an intense, fresh structure that mixes fruit, tannins and oak in a harmonious, silky whole. Nicolas' work here was rewarded when the château was upgraded to a Premier Grand Cru Classé in the 2012 classification of Saint-Emilion.

Nicolas, ably assisted by his winemaking son Cyrille, who is also managing L'If for his uncle Jacques, is today also overseeing the wine at Château Beauséjour Duffau-Lagarrosse and Château Larcis Ducasse, which, after 10 years of Nicolas' management, was promoted, like Château Pavie Macquin, to Premier Grand Cru Classé in the 2012 Saint-Emilion classification.

Nicolas is truly the 'thinker' of the family with a hundred and one projects turning in his head. He has a quick, lively intelligence, is keen to share his new techniques and ideas with his cousins or anyone else who is interested, and has become known as one of Bordeaux's best and most exciting winemakers. Nicolas' rare moments of relaxation at the coast in Arcachon allow him to ponder on his achievements and think about the challenges ahead. 'When we managed finally to make some money for Pavie Macquin by selling the wine on the Bordeaux market I realized that I was capable of doing some good work,' he tells me modestly.

It is quite rare to find three cousins working in close proximity to each other on such a large variety of estates and the nearness does help to firm up family ties within the different branches of the family. What is really heartening to see, is that all three of them are nurturing the careers of the next generation: Alexandre with his son Guillaume at Vieux Château Certan; Jacques with his two nephews: Maxime at his new project L'Hêtre in the Côtes de Castillon, and Alexander who has joined the wine merchant business in Etikhove, the sixth generation to work there; and Nicolas with Cyrille. All three feel that tutoring the next cohort of winemakers keeps them young and gives them an enormous sense of pride. Time will tell if our two sons will join them. They are currently both at university and we have told them we would like them to study as much as they want and get work experience elsewhere before they decide to join the family wine business. It has not always been easy being what family members call '*la pièce rapportée*' (the addition) although sometimes I'm granted the title of '*valeur ajoutée*' (additional asset) among the Thienponts, whose pride in their family heritage can verge on arrogance. Like other spouses, I have had to fight my corner on several occasions if I have wanted to play an active role in the family business, but there is no denying the rewards that it has brought.

While there are obviously the occasional complications and tensions between members of such a large family, especially with regard to Vieux Château Certan, there is a deep feeling of legacy running through each of them; a feeling that you will see quite often with other wine families. The last word goes to Cyrille Thienpont. 'Being a Thienpont is both a privilege and a responsibility. We are linked to a history that began a long time ago; our name makes certain things easier and opens lots of doors, but above all, we have to be worthy of our heritage.'

Harvest hands

Fiona pouring at a Le Pin harvest lunch

Fiona's favourite Thienpont wines

Château Puygueraud

The wines of the Côtes de Francs and Castillon offer such great value and are rich, spicy and satisfying. Puygueraud always has notes of black cherries, plums and a dark spicy backbone. I love its personality and its sheer drinkability, even when young.

L'If

My husband, Jacques, bought this estate right next to Château Troplong Mondot in 2010 (where grandfather Georges bought his first château). Made by Cyrille Thienpont, the wine just gets better and better and shows beautiful glossy, damson fruit, lovely purity and fresh juicy flavours underlain by richness and structure.

Vieux Château Certan

This wine just continues to improve, and is now really at the top of its game. There are red fruit flavours and fresh notes of mango in the lifted fruit, plus a beautiful elegance and silky texture. A lovely intensity of flavour and a long, echo of fruit, truffle and cedary oak mark the finish. So elegant; so classy: the quintessential Pomerol.

Pavie Macquin

This château has a really great situation on top of the Saint-Emilion plateau. A trio of majestic oaks marks the highest point of the vineyard and one was the village's hanging tree, hence the rather ominous noose on the wine's label. When young, Pavie Macquin has very ripe, sweet oaky, quite concentrated flavours, but with eight to 10 years ageing the wine mellows out to become warm, generous, blackberry scented and velvety with beautiful precision and freshness.

Le Pin

Jacques and I joke that we only drink Le Pin out of the barrel because once it is bottled it is beyond our means. In spite of its youthful exuberance and its rich mocha and red cherry flavours, the wine ages incredibly beautifully, especially in cooler years, to reveal a Burgundian purity, silkiness and freshness that even after all these years surprises us with its beauty.

Alvaro the bullfighter

Ricardo Perez, lover of the 'calm' wines of cool Bierzo

Coruña, landing on a wet and rainy Saturday in a small Galician town that promises little. I meet up with photographer Alexandre James and we set out for Bierzo, heading southeast on the newly built motorway. (I am impressed as I travel through Spain and Portugal to see how EU money has been spent on improving the roads in these two countries.)

We pass signs marking the sites of old gold mines and notice abandoned mineshafts on the sides of the road. We see the scallop shell sign of Saint James marking the route to Compostela and take a detour to visit the ancient village of Cacabelos, the scent of wood smoke mingling with the damp bracken and stone. In the autumn mist, a few pilgrims are still passing through the village, which is welcoming and comforting in spite of the dark granite of the buildings, the shiny wet paving stones and the lurking grey clouds. As I so often do when visiting historic sites, I let myself imagine the lives and souls belonging to the feet that have trodden this path throughout the centuries. It is a wonder that in the technological age in which we live, the 'Camino' is more popular today than it has ever been.

That evening, we meet up with Ricardo Perez, son of Chelo, Alvaro's sister who runs the family hotel built by her husband right next to the winery in Alfaro. Ricardo has one of those faces that you instantly warm to. Round and lively with dancing aqua blue eyes behind thick black-rimmed Ray-Ban glasses, a cherubic face framed by a mop of unruly black curls and dark sideburns, he greets us with big hugs. Like his uncle, he too studied oenology in Bordeaux and did an apprenticeship in the vineyards of Pomerol before moving to Bierzo in 1998 aged 24.

Alvaro's daughter, Lola, is still at university, so in the meantime, Alvaro is passing on his knowledge to Ricardo, 11 years his junior, and revelling in his enthusiasm and energy, just as Jacques Thienpont is currently doing in Bordeaux with his nephews Cyrille and Maxime.

We have dinner at the Moncloa de San Lazaro, one of the *posadas* on the Camino. It is an old inn full of wine, hearty food, music, warmth and joy. Ricardo opens a bottle of La Faraona ('the pharaoh's wife') 2015, the mythical wine of Bierzo. It is his best vintage to date and as the wine warms in the glass, it buzzes with life and throws up aromas of violets and vanilla, pata negra ham and roasted walnuts. There is great silkiness and freshness here in spite of the warm vintage. Later, as the evening moves on, a sultry singer provokes a more contemplative mood and Ricardo opens a bottle of the Las Lamas 2009; here ripe cherry fruit mixes with dark chocolate flavours and herbs such as thyme and rosemary.

Ricardo talks about the reasons for settling in this rather forlorn corner of Spain, especially since he and his companion Paula, who works in far-away Jerez, have a newly born baby girl, Jara. 'When I came back to Alfaro after my studies in France, there wasn't really a place for me. In France I learned about organic farming and I really wanted to make organic wines. I went to talk to Alvaro and told him that I had found this great region where the soil and climate meant that I could make cooler climate wines, calm wines.'

Alvaro knew the region well as one of his activities in the past was to sell barrels throughout Spain in order to raise money for his Priorat project. To begin with, in 1998, just to make sure that they knew what they were doing, the pair bought grapes from different parcels of old vines and rented a cellar in the middle of Bierzo. Alvaro was familiar with the schist soils found here since they were similar to those in Priorat where he had started to make wine several years earlier.

Next morning, we begin to explore the region. The village of Bierzo harks back to its days as an old mining town, now almost empty and poor. As far back as Roman times the region was known for its wine and its gold. Later, the road to Compostela became its lifeblood, the vital vein bringing people through the hills. We walk along the country paths, which are sodden and heavy from last night's rain. We hear the shots of the hunters hoping to bag a wild boar. Dogs bark in small gardens. As the pale sun lifts off the damp earth, wisps of steamy clouds stray across the hills and pick out the ochre, yellow and orange tones of the vine leaves. Vines are grown on the southern slopes while the northern slopes are planted with cherry and chestnut trees.

It is the meeting point of the Atlantic and the Mediterranean climates, and the two single vineyards of Las Lamas and Moncerbal illustrate this beautifully: Las Lamas' wine is made on the Atlantic side of the valley with more clay in the soil and is spicy and fruity; Moncerbal is made on the Mediterranean side and has great energy and sweetness and is round and generous. The vineyards are found in the village of Corullón and the principal

At the top of the famous Faraona vineyard, its wines revered as Bierzo's answer to burgundy

grape here is Mencía: a local red variety with beautiful fruit expression but low acidity that, as Ricardo tells me, 'has to be picked on exactly the right day'.

The jewel in the vineyard crown is La Faraona, a name that everyone locally says in a sort of reverential whisper. Situated at 950 metres on average, this steep, rocky, arid, southeast-facing vineyard is covered with bush vines, around 70 years old. Small pieces of shale and quartz lie on top of a bedrock of schist. At the top of the parcel, the wind whistles around the hills, rustling the remaining leaves. The wine tastes of its soil: earthy, warm, pure and expressive with lively notes of cherry and pomegranate, a burgundy in Bierzo. Ricardo tells me how pleased the previous owner – an old bachelor whose love of his life was his vines – is to hear that his vineyard has become world famous.

Today, there are 700 hectares of vines in the appellation and the region is regarded as one of Spain's most exciting. Palacios owns 45 hectares but included in this are trees and scrubland. 'It is very important to continue polyculture here,' Ricardo tells me. 'This is the more human sense of farming and we are improving the landscape at the same time.' Clearing scrubland, tending orchards and raising goats is also part of the way to make great wine here. All this comes at a price. For example, to plant a single hectare of 3,000 vines it takes a week of working by hand. There are 15 people working full time in the vineyards and the yields are pitifully low.

Ricardo's biodynamic farming methods also play a major role. Seven mules and horses work 30 hectares of land and at the farm where Ricardo lives he has started a school where lessons are given in bread making, winemaking, cheese making, organic farming, painting and even Japanese calligraphy. In the classroom, he has a collection of fossils and minerals that he gathered during walks with his grandfather when he was a boy.

If you haven't heard about biodynamics, it is probably a good idea that I stop for a moment to talk about it. Many of the winemakers in this book practise biodynamic farming in some way or other and several, such as Palacios, Müller, Liger-Belair and Perrin, are fully committed. Biodynamics is based on the theories of Rudolph Steiner, a philosopher and scientist living in the early 20th century in Germany. Steiner focused on the life of the soil, fertility, plant growth and animal management as part of a holistic, organic whole, using natural preparations and sprays based on herbs, composts, manures and minerals. These can vary from infusions made out of nettles, chamomile or dandelion to cow manure buried in horns and quartz. The treatments are prepared using a spinning vortex and then sprayed in the vineyards using very small doses. It reminds me a bit of homeopathic medicine. In biodynamics, choosing the right moment to prune, sow, plough or pick is determined by the positions of the sun and the moon and how nature's forces are influenced by the four elements of air, fire, water and earth.

If this all sounds like a lot of hocus-pocus, go and spend some time in a vineyard where biodynamics is used. The first thing you will notice is the life in the soil and in the flora and fauna around. At a time when climate change is preoccupying every farmer, it is also a way of countering the excesses of drought and heat. Secondly, the respect for nature and for polyculture is evident. It is a counter movement to the industrialized, mechanical, chemical side of farming.

I also believe that as a new generation of winemakers inherited its vineyards around the late 1980s and 1990s, the time was ripe for organic farming and biodynamic ideas caught the imagination. The parents of this new generation in Europe had worked their land after World War II when the major chemical companies pumped huge amounts of their synthetic products into agriculture. Even as late as the mid-1980s, I remember a calendar sponsored by one of the big chemical companies that was pre-printed with the dates when the crops should be treated and sprayed, hanging in the office. Today, this is an anathema to many and every great estate practises some form of sustainable farming. The move to ban pesticides is just one good result of this movement.

As we walk the land, Ricardo talks about balance. 'We should aim to influence the vineyards as little as possible; the wines should reflect the true character of the region,' he insists. 'As we get to know the land, the soil and the climate better, we adapt our winemaking to each vintage, so that the wine is true to that year.' The social aspect is also very important to him. He tries to get young farmers interested in his courses so that they will be inspired to improve their grapes and he hopes that they will follow his example to help keep the region alive. One of the key steps in this direction has been the classifying of Bierzo vineyard parcels in 2017, making this the first region to be officially recognized under the new legislation which maps out the great vineyard sites of Spain.

We stop to visit a local grape grower in Hornija from whom Ricardo buys grapes for the Pétalos wine. He is given a huge welcome and we are ushered into the small wooden cellar. The farmer draws a jug of the freshly made wine from an old barrel and it splashes carmine coloured and violet scented into our rough beakers. His wife carves us hunks of delicious bread freshly baked in the village's communal oven, the perfect Sunday Eucharist.

You can spot the new DJP (Descendientes de J Palacios) winery from far off. It stands as a fortress on a hill above Corullón, made of concrete tinted to the colour of the local stone, with local chestnut wood used throughout and enormous picture windows looking out over the landscape. A gorgeously symmetrical spiral staircase descends to the barrel cellar where the local rock forms the outside wall. Everywhere is clean, elegant and quite majestic and it has the same design ethos as Alvaro's cellar in Priorat.

As Ricardo shows me the new cellar, we both laugh at the evident signs of Alvaro Palacios' maniacal attention to detail – the curve of a stair, the office furniture, the placement of the window, the polish of the doors. To give the wines the right balance between richness and freshness, one quarter of the grapes are put into the vats as whole bunches, trodden down to release their juice, and then the rest of the harvest – the now destemmed berries – is added on top. When aged in oak, the taste of the wood never overwhelms the wine but is used as a frame around a work of art.

The new state of the art winery is impressive. There is light but there is also gravitas; there is space but there are also small corners of the winery where a few experimental barrels are left to age quietly. It is all a very far cry from the old, musty cellar in the centre of Bierzo with its dirt floor and myriad cobwebs that I first visited a decade ago. This reminds me of the transition my husband, Jacques, made from the tiny little basement shed to the grown-up, spacious winery at Le Pin, and I realize that almost all the great wines I know, whether in Bordeaux, Burgundy, the Mosel or in Piedmont, began in modest sheds or basements.

Ricardo talks with such respect and affection about Alvaro that you can feel the energy and the propulsion he receives from his uncle, who pushes him to new levels. Ricardo may preach the bible of biodynamics but it is Alvaro who has channelled his instinctive skills to great use. They make a great team.

The soaring architecture of Alvaro Palacios' cellar in Priorat

Ricardo Perez with the new Bierzo winery in the background

It is three o'clock in the afternoon and Alexandre James and I had both been getting hungry – not for the first time, I cursed the timing of Spanish meals. We finish our visit to Bierzo with a wonderful Sunday lunch surrounded by families spanning several generations. To my surprise, darkness is falling when we finally emerge from the restaurant; as we leave I feel a great affection for Ricardo and his connection to the old lands of this region. Filled with further tastes of Las Lamas and Moncerbal and copious quantities of roast goat and country hams and cheeses, I am grateful that I don't have to do the driving as we travel southeast through the countryside back to Rioja.

When we arrive in Alfaro several hours later, I feel as if we have been zapped forward by at least a half a century into the modern, colourful, brightly lit town. Alvaro and Cristina are there to meet us and we have a cosy late Sunday evening supper together.

At home in Rioja

Smallish but lithe, dark, with slightly greying hair and piercing pale blue eyes, Alvaro is ruggedly handsome with a magnetism that draws you instinctively to him. He can win over an amphitheatre of wine lovers or the wine critic tasting his wines one on one. He is fiercely loyal and surprisingly quite private, but the word that most accurately describes him is 'passionate': his passion for his family and especially his wife Cristina and daughter Lola, for his wines but especially his vineyards, and for his close circle of friends is wonderful to behold. His big frustration today is that he is pulled in so many directions, with so many projects filling his head that he sometimes makes mistakes or errors of judgement that will affect him for a while. When possible, Cristina, beautiful, blond and warm hearted, is at his side to calm his nerves and bring a sense of stability to his life.

As I wait for him the next morning, Alexandre James and I look around the charming family museum in the basement of the hotel, looking for clues to his past. Alvaro's bullfighting cape is there, as are some of his father's fossils. Lots of photographs attest to how wine was made by the previous

critics are right. I don't really care if it conforms or not because the wine is delicious, silky, fresh and fruity. It is so quaffable that I forget to really concentrate on its aromas of wild herbs, its soft, ripe fruit and the notes of wood smoke, minerals and dried meats on the finish. This is a great wine that can easily take its place alongside La Faraona and L'Ermita. We talk about the three sites and Alvaro points out that each has its own type of nut: Bierzo has chestnuts, Alfaro has almonds and Priorat has hazelnuts. It is the sort of nugget of information that Alvaro drops into your notebook every now and then.

Priorat

Later that evening, we leave Rioja for Priorat with Alvaro and Cristina, and we spend the next four hours listening to Flamenco music in the car. Luckily Alvaro drives fast but the journey is long and, however much I love local colour, I am relieved when we arrive in Falset. I've spent many an evening with Alvaro and friends that invariably ends with him playing the guitar and singing expressive Flamenco, but this has been rather too intensive a dose. Cristina smiles sweetly when I grumble a bit to her. Over dinner we shift gears and I ask Alvaro to tell me once again the tale of Gratallops.

'When I returned from abroad, totally infected by the French philosophy and the notion of *terroir*, I was 24 years old. Spain was just beginning to open up in the 1980s after 40 years of isolation. I felt that there would be lots of *"grand cru"* vineyards to discover but found that Rioja was too industrial.' In Bordeaux, Alvaro's brother Antonio shared a house with René Barbier, a Catalonian with Burgundian roots. To cut a long story short, 'René became my second mentor after my father', Alvaro explains. 'It was he who got me the job at Petrus,' he adds, with reference to Pomerol's famous wine. René told Alvaro about a little vineyard he had in Priorat, and Alvaro became intrigued by the idea of making wine there. He joined a group of slightly hippy, slightly crazy wine growers centred around the tiny village of Gratallops who pooled their resources to share winemaking facilities and began in 1989 to rent or buy up small parcels of old vines.

Priorat, like all of Spain's wine regions except for Rioja, had been forgotten and the forest had reclaimed many of the terraces that had been created in the past. It had been popular for its good climate and llicorella soils. Although it is hot during the summer the coast is only 20 kilometres away and sea breezes plus the high altitude help keep the soils cool. The soils are of volcanic origin with mica, silica, slate and granite, and with the high acidity levels so excellent for vines. Yet, sadly, vineyard plantings had decreased from over 5,000 hectares to a pitiful 600 in 1989. Thanks to the great success of the wines produced here today, however, Priorat is now back to 1,700 hectares of vines.

Why did Alvaro fall for this region with its wild, rocky landscape? Partly it was the challenge of resurrecting a land that had grown grapes since the Middle Ages but had been abandoned during the Civil War. Partly it may have been the historic presence of the Carthusian monks at the Abbey of Scala Dei. And partly it was the sheer independence of this region that the world had forgotten.

Alvaro was the youngest in the Gratallops group and was nicknamed the Dolphin so the wine he made was called Clos Dofi (using the Catalan word for dolphin). The wines were all named 'Clos' to emphasize the importance of the vineyard sites and were a dark purple colour, wild smelling, with aromas of rock, herbs and very intense blackberry and blackcurrant fruit. The wines caught the attention of international wine critics, who loved the intensity and the richness of the flavours. Soon, Alvaro had the money to invest in more land and begun planting vineyards and buying up parcels of old Garnacha bush vines that he found in the hills surrounding the village. One day in 1993 – in circumstances similar to those with the Faraona parcel in Bierzo – he had the chance to buy a steep 1.4-hectare northeast-facing vineyard that lay under a tiny sanctuary called L'Ermita. The Garnacha vines were almost 100 years old and at an altitude of up to 500 metres. 'It can be like an iceberg up there in winter,' he laughs.

'A great wine should be spiritual, transcendent; it should be able to fly beyond its physical attributes to touch your soul,' Alvaro pronounces as we pile into his jeep for a tour of the vineyards. He believes that for a wine to be truly great, it should have a heritage, a history from which it springs. This can be an ancient parcel of abandoned vines pared out of the steep granite

Fiona's favourite Palacios wines

Moncerbal – Bierzo

Born on the schist and limestone slopes of Corullón, made from the Mencía grape, this wine has great freshness and acidity as well as structure. Very precise with wonderful crunchy cherry fruit, great purity and length with lots of character.

Corullón – Bierzo

I once did a vertical tasting of every vintage of Corullón and was struck by the intensity of the fruit and the pretty floral, violet notes. On the palate the wine is quite powerful and tannic when young but with age it smooths out to become spicy, round, pure and balanced with good sweetness. Have a look also at Pétalos for an everyday drinking Mencía wine.

Quiñón de Valmira – Rioja Orientale

Challenges any ideas you might have had in the past about Rioja. The zenith of Garnacha grown at high altitude with restraint and minerality, this wine has fruit, depth and silkiness, all beautifully in balance. Quintessentially Spanish but with the Palacios touch.

Les Aubaguetes – Priorat

A north-facing single vineyard site producing very old Garnacha vines. This very expressive wine smells of warm stones, figs, sloes and dried herbs. It is sweet and fresh and beautifully silky. On the end of the palate, you feel the power of the tannins.

L'Ermita – Priorat

Born with a sacred name, the purity of the fruit and the freshness is what strikes you first. On the nose there is a touch of fennel, red cherry and pomegranate. Then the wine opens up further to reveal depths of spicy flavour with great intensity and length.

Grandfather Eduard Marius, collector of books, coins, stamps and occasionally port

Niepoort Ports & Wines

A varietal uprising in the Douro

He paces back and forth. Pulls out his mobile, punches in his code, stares at the screen. It is blank. He stares again, willing it to come to life. Nothing. He thrusts it back into his jeans pocket. And begins pacing again. Ten minutes later, the phone vibrates. He yanks at it. Reads a text from his lawyer. Barks a laugh and thrusts the phone back into his jeans. This has been going on for the three days that I am in Portugal and God knows how long before I had arrived. Dirk Niepoort is involved in a battle, a rather public one, with his sister, Verena, over the future of the family company. I have arrived in the eye of the storm.

The trouble began when Dirk and Verena's parents decided to divide the company between their two children. Dirk, active in the company since 1987 and responsible for saving its fortunes with the introduction of table wines, was given a few more shares than his sister in recognition of his work. This sparked off a sibling rivalry that has gradually escalated over the years. For Dirk, the only solution is to buy his sister's shares, but at what price?

This book is centred on the current generations of 10 great winemaking families. Each one has had and still has family tensions that flow through the generations. Ensuring the survival of a wine estate is never easy, especially since the wine business is so dependent upon the vagaries of climate. The financial difference between a great and a poor vintage can run into millions of euros. How a company creates a buffer zone to cope with these vagaries is often the key to its survival. Where money is combined with ego, conflicts arise easily. No family is spared, but the ways that the protagonists featured here are dealing with these problems adds a further, quite intimate dimension to the portraits of these fascinating dynasties.

From Hilversum to Oporto

The Niepoort port dynasty began when Franciscus Marius van der Niepoort, who was born in Hilversum in Holland in 1813, moved to Portugal in 1842 and started a business as a port merchant with no land or vineyards. His company prospered slowly through the next three generations and Dirk remembers his grandfather Eduard Marius being more interested in collecting books, coins and stamps than in port. With each generation, there has been an overlap so that father and son work together for several years. Dirk's father, Rolf, had good business sense and began working with his own father in the 1960s, steering the company through a difficult post-war period and making good relationships both commercially and with the grape growers. Like his father before him, Rolf is a great collector – especially of old Portuguese weapons and vintage cars.

Born in 1964, Dirk is pretty much self-taught. He didn't go to oenology college but having gone to school in Oporto, he studied business in Switzerland, worked at Swiss wine merchant Mövenpick and at the Cuvaison winery in California's Napa Valley. He learned the trade on the job, joining the family company in 1987 at the age of 23, working alongside his father, whom he clearly adores. Rolf retired in 2005 and celebrated his 90th birthday in 2017. Strong faced with thick grey hair and wire spectacles, Rolf still has a firm jaw, bright eyes and an inquisitive mind, even if these days he is confined to a wheelchair. Dirk is the fifth generation to run the company but the first family member to actually make wine and port himself. Daniel, his eldest son, is working in the Mosel in Germany on the FIO project, while Marco, his second son, has just started to

Dirk decanting an old Madeira at home

work helping co-ordinate the wines at Quinta de Nápoles. They represent the sixth generation of the Niepoort family. Interestingly, all of the Niepoort men have Germanic wives. Dirk's mother is German and the three other most important women in his life are German speaking. His first wife was Swiss, his second Austrian and his third, Nina, with whom he has spent the last 11 years, is German from near Cologne. His English is perfect, idiomatic. He is a citizen of the world; he has a Dutch passport but has never lived there; he feels Portuguese, but doesn't look Portuguese. His mother tongue is German.

As soon as you set eyes on Dirk, you know that he is an original, a personality to be reckoned with. Stocky and of medium height, he has worn the same clothes almost since I first met him: checked cotton shirts; a fisherman's beige cotton vest with lots of pockets, a paper-clip attached to one of them; jeans, and on his feet, a pair of Crocs plastic sandals. His hair circles his face in a ring of unruly, cascading waves and his intelligent blue eyes are encased in wire rim glasses. He is one of the most perceptive and intuitive people I know, summing up people quickly and correctly. He thinks before he speaks, is not afraid to leave a gap in the conversation, but can also be prone to off the cuff outbursts, especially at this tense, emotional time. He has, in his own words, a built-in 'bullshit-ometer' and his eyes can glaze over if visitors resort to clichés and platitudes. There is something of the virtuoso about him; a vinous acrobat who is capable of making both the brooding Batuta and the elegant Charme wines. Don't be fooled by the Boho exterior. Dirk gets involved in every step of production – from making and ageing the wine to selling and marketing it. Here is a clear-headed businessman, eager to seize any commercial opportunity. It is hard to overestimate his impact on the Douro.

Dirk has been running the company for the last 20 years, and everything went quite smoothly until it was time to talk about the succession. His parents decided to split the company between their two children. Later, Verena started working in the company coming up with marketing ideas and, as Dirk says it, 'various nutty schemes'. All this might seem logical enough until you learn who exactly Dirk Niepoort is. Put succinctly, he is the hero of the Douro. Dirk has been the driving force behind a certain style of table wine made from indigenous grapes. He is a brilliant communicator who has been able to understand and highlight the great assets of the Douro through his wines. Although there were a few producers who made table wine in the Douro before he came along (Ferreira's Barca Velha is a famous example), he is the most visible of the winemakers who have saved the fortunes of local grape growers by making wine rather than port. Not that he turned his back on port – the Niepoort family is one of the oldest and most established houses and is especially known for its Garrafeira and Colheita ports – but as port became less fashionable, he found another outlet for the grapes grown in the Douro. He argues, with justification, that he has been single-handedly responsible for saving the fortunes of the family company and turning it into the best-known and second largest producer of wines in Portugal. His sister demurs. You can quickly understand why temperatures have risen so high over the last few months. The move to producing wines saved the company but also indirectly provoked the family drama that is unfolding today.

We have dinner at Dirk's home on the outskirts of Oporto that he shares with Nina Gruntkowski. Nina was a German journalist who specialized in Brazil and in the Portuguese-speaking countries of Africa. When she arrived in Oporto, a friend told her to contact Dirk. For the first 15 minutes of their conversation they talked Portuguese until they both realized that their mother tongues were German. Nina is not in the wine business, and Dirk laughs with relief: 'Finally, someone who likes me for myself.'

Nina's passion lies in another crop, not unlike grapes, and that is tea. Dirk shares her enthusiasm and they recently fulfiled a dream of creating a small tea plantation. Tea is made from a species of the Camellia plant and near where they live is an area called the 'land of the Camellias'. They started by planting 200 tea seedlings in their garden in 2011. When, five years later, the tea plants were ready for their first harvest, they realized that this was a viable project. Dirk and Nina have now produced Portugal's first green tea and import a range of delicate, subtle teas from small growers in Japan. Their tea is called Pipacha and is a nod to the port barrels, called pipes, in which the leaves are aged. We talk about teas and laugh about the similarities between wine and tea – how climate and *terroir* play such a big role, how the tea is brewed, at what temperature it is served and in what shape of cup. Like many wine producers, the arrival of Asian wine buyers in Europe has opened up our tastebuds to the wonderful subtle world of tea, as they often bring examples with them when they visit our wine estates. Over the years, we have begun to

Nina and Dirk at home

Dirk's kitchen, like his life, is a hotbed of experiments and ideas

Dirk Niepoort, philosopher and optimist

home for the company's extraordinary collection of Colheitas and Garrafeiras. Niepoort is famous for these two types of port. A Colheita is an aged tawny port from a specific vintage. By law, the port must be aged for seven years before bottling but Niepoort keeps its Colheitas for several more years in barrel. As the port ages in old wooden barrels, it takes on a golden, burnished copper colour. Once bottled, it can last for years and I am incredibly touched when later that day, at lunchtime, Dirk opens a Colheita from my birth year that was aged in barrel for 20 years. It is extraordinarily silky and fine on the palate with wonderful flavours of walnuts, figs and cedar wood. 'The best ports in the world,' Dirk exclaims. Niepoort is known for its Colheitas, a category that the English port houses rather ignored, although now they are actively promoting them.

Even more impressive are the Garrafeiras, aged in large demijohns that came from an apothecary in Germany. These were purchased by the second generation of the family in the late 19th century and have a capacity of between eight and 12 litres. There are around 4,000 of them lined up on shelves in the cellar below. Dirk's grandfather first used them in 1931 for the

The large demijohns used for making the Niepoort Garrafeiras

best port selection of the vintage. They are hard to manage and very fragile and Dirk's father was all set to give them up until Dirk decided to give them another chance in 1987. 'It was the first good thing I did,' he says with a smile.

There is something sacred about these large glass jars and the opening of one of them is a ritual, a special moment treasured by family and friends. The jars have a very small opening for the cork and on purpose are only filled to the shoulder level so that air can be trapped inside. It takes at least 20 years for one of these special bottlings to come onto the market. We taste the 1977, which is seamless, beautiful, fresh and silky. There is a sense of drinking history as the faded fruit yields its soft nutty, cedar and slightly salty tastes. They seem burgundian to me; elegant, a touch savoury, with Christmas spices and raisins.

This impressive cellar is also the scene of a large, underground dining room, albeit in need of a good dusting off. Here Dirk invites the 600 or so grape growers that he works with for a good lunch once a year. Niepoort does not have contracts with any of them. Dirk follows his instincts and makes sure that in his dealings, there is an advantage for both parties. 'With the wines, everything is new,' he concludes, 'but with port, I'm not going to change the world, there are just a few little touches'. I ask him which he prefers, wine or port, and a fleeting look of irritation sweeps across his face as if I had asked him which of his children he prefers: 'I feel as involved with the ports as the wine. The finest port I have ever made is the 2015 vintage,' he states emphatically.

Projectos

We step out again into the narrow street. I feel like Alice stepping back through the looking glass and I have to admit, my visit to the new Niepoort cellars and offices on the Rua Cândido dos Reis is somewhat of a disappointment in that it seems so normal. We pass by the office, pausing to shake the hand of sister Verena, who takes pains to greet us while at the same time managing to ignore the presence of her brother completely. In the cellar, we meet Rodrigo Nogueira, the fifth generation of the same family of master blenders to have worked with the Niepoorts since they began here in 1842. Rodrigo was the first member of his family to get an oenology degree in Viña Real before he joined the winery in 2006. He worked alongside his father, José Nogueira, until 2011 when José retired, unwilling, his son explains, to face the stress of learning about all the new wines. 'Niepoort has changed tremendously in the last 10 years,' he says. 'It's amazing because we know that Dirk is always coming up with something new.'

As we tour the vast cellars with their stainless steel vats like tall pillars and their impressive oak casks, I try to keep tabs on the different ports that are made here. Apart from the traditional line up of white, ruby and tawny ports of various ages, I come across bottles with white fairy tale-like figures painted on them. 'Ah, those are the Niepoortland ports,' Rodrigo explains: a series of Lewis Carroll-inspired figures including Ruby Dum and Tawny Dee and the White Rabbit, a dry white port. The fables continue, this time with two naughty little boys, Max and Moritz, the creations of 19th-century German author Wilhelm Busch. Someone is obviously enjoying themselves in here and I'm sure you can guess who.

As we turn the corner into another part of the cellar, I find the same zany array of names for a wine that is bottled according to each export market, each with a different name and design; a logistical nightmare for the warehouse team. Cartoon characters dance and play in labels looking like perforated stamps with names such as Diálog for Portugal, Allez Santé for Belgium, Eto Carta for Japan, Drink Me for the UK and Twisted for the USA. There is a method to the madness: over a million bottles are sold of all these wines and ports, which are intended to be playful, drinkable and accessible, designed for a younger market when port drinkers are fading fast.

We drive to a hip restaurant, Gaveto, in Matosinhos to the west of Porto for lunch. This long-established restaurant is undergoing major refurbishment so we are treated to a sort of pop-up while the builders are working around us. Gaveto is Dirk's dining room where he and other port shippers can bring their own wine. Dirk's mother joins us, although sadly his father is too weak to come too. In spite of the family tensions, we have a good lunch and Dirk has brought along some of his 'projectos' wines. This is Dirk in his mad professor role – wildly experimenting either with unusual grape varieties in the Douro or wines that he has made as collaborations with other winemakers. Many of these names I know and respect: Telmo Rodriguez and Raúl Pérez from Spain, Dorli Muhr, Dirk's ex-wife from Austria, and Eben Sadie from South Africa. The idea of Dirk reaching over frontiers in joint ventures really appeals to me and my belief that the wine business is a better place thanks to the global exchange of ideas.

We taste a 2013 'B', which stands for Bical, an unusual grape variety grown at high altitudes on north-facing slopes. Made without sulphur and aged in 1,000 litre barrels it is dark golden in colour, with good ripe fruit, salty intensity and is very 'full on'. Next comes a Calderera 2011 made with Raúl Pérez from Mencía grapes and fermented on the skins. It is aged in old port barrels and tastes rich, wild and cherry flavoured. One of the most fairy tale wines is called Turris made from one ancient vine, totally untrained, planted over 130 years ago deep in the heart of the Douro region. The wine is sexy, big and ripe with sweet plummy fruit; youthful tasting in spite of the vine's old age and moving into a powerful reverberation, like a drum roll, on the finish. I pick up the bottle with its pink capsule and its artistic squiggly label. 'This doesn't seem like you,' I tell Dirk. 'No, it isn't. No, yes, it is because it's not me,' he replies. 'Then who is it?' I think to myself quizzically.

Finally, we taste a 2014 'D' (named for his son Daniel) made at Quinta de Baixo in Bairrada, Dirk's vineyard in the area. The wine has lots of personality, is light and fresh with soft grapey fruit sprinkled with pepper. It is not a certainty that all of these wines will make it to the wider market; they are 'projects' to stimulate Dirk's brain cells and tastebuds. One of the wines, Clos de Crappe, has the following tasting note from Dirk: 'A modern old style wine. A wine full of character, some mistakes. Technically a disaster. But a wine full of passion and expression. A wild, intense nose full of reduction. A palate "the incredible lightness of being". Fine, elegant and very long. What the hell is Clos de Crappe?'

Dirk Niepoort is having fun and it throws a lighter touch of comedy on the somewhat darker family drama. Incessant calls between lawyers are going on around us as each sibling tries to bargain their corner. Not for the first time, Dirk has been led to believe that his sister is ready to sign the deeds of sale, only to have those hopes dashed by another clause or complication.

highlight the production of fine wines made with small yields, modern winemaking techniques and the best local grapes. There are five producers in the group and it has gained plaudits around the world, throwing new light on this incredibly beautiful, classic wine region. I do think, however, that some of the other producers have something to learn from Dirk since many Douro wines still seem very dry, tannic and hard, and I'm astonished at the prices these wines fetch, often well over €100 a bottle.

When I ask Dirk if there is a different winemaking philosophy for wine versus port, he casts me a slightly withering look. 'Come on,' he admonishes me, 'it's much more complicated than that. In the Douro you have such a difference in altitude (from eight to 800 metres), a difference in exposures (the direction that the vineyards face) and over 80 different grape varieties. There are vineyards destined for port and those that are better suited for wine'. Rather like Palacios in Spain, he is in favour of north-facing, high altitude parcels for wine. Port is less difficult to grow than wine in that it takes the excesses of weather and climate change in its stride. With more than 45,000 hectares of vines, there certainly seems to be room for both wine and port.

Before I leave the Douro I ask Dirk how he can run a business and yet live with a certain studied chaos. (I am thinking of his wine cellar at home and the jungle of cartons left abandoned by the bottling site in the old cellar in Vila Nova de Gaia.) He shrugs his shoulders and says: 'I'm not organized but I'm good at ideas' – one of the rare understatements of my visit. As we near the airport, we come into satellite contact and Dirk's phone buzzes and rings with messages. 'Don't worry,' he reassures me, 'I think we are very close to working out a deal'. I am sad, because I really did hope that the future of the company would be settled while I was there, as Dirk had promised when I arrived.

A month or so later, on Christmas Eve, I get this message: 'I just finally got the perfect Christmas present: "things" with my sister have finally come to an end, papers all signed and all sorted out. I will run the company and must confess to feeling a huge relief.' And the icing on the cake, as I am writing this chapter, is another message that comes in: his son Marco is joining him at Quinta de Nápoles and the final deeds were signed on 15 February 2018.

I do love happy endings!

Dirk, in his famous fisherman's vest, arrives with port to sample

Fiona's favourite Niepoort wines and ports

Coche
Old vines, high altitude, biodynamic farming, this wine has a difficult to define nose of citrus, minerals, white blossom and warm rocks. Firm, lively and elegant with an almost salty flavour, it opens up on the palate to reveal dried fruits, oak and citrus. A serious white wine worthy of a great burgundy.

Charme
For me this is what Douro table wines should taste like. Made in stone *lagares* with all of the stems intact, it has all the fruity flavours of a ruby port – juicy plums, spice, a touch of dark chocolate – but is a fresh, perfectly balanced dry wine with a great, soft, generous finish.

Turris
I haven't seen the very old, sprawling vine that makes this wine in the centre of the Douro but you can feel the age and the concentration in the wild floral, herbal fruity aromas and the mineral intensity. Brilliant dark purple colour, ripe and very attractive.

Niepoort Colheita Port
You should try to find a Niepoort Colheita from a vintage that reminds you of an important event since there are quite a lot of different years on the market. The port is tawny coloured, very suave and fresh with notes of almonds, fresh figs, cedar and a touch of orange peel. Very, very persistent in the finish.

Niepoort 2015 Vintage Port
A perfect vintage according to Niepoort: perfectly ripe grapes with full, generous tannins, the port is still sweet and fresh with lovely cool plummy flavours. It is silky yet generous with great length and precision and I can see this evolving slowly over the years to be a real classic.

WINTER

Gaja
Barbaresco, Italy

One man towers over all Italian wines. Thirty years ago he forced wine
drinkers to sit up and taste the beauty of his wines when most people's image
of Italy was insipid red wine in straw covered bottles. The world of wine was
never the same again and yet Angelo Gaja says his greatest achievement is
having his three talented children working with him and his wife, Lucia.

Egon Müller
Scharzhofberg, Mosel, Germany

This is a story as much about a vineyard as a family. Perched high up above
the River Mosel, its slopes so steep that you need to be a mountain goat to
traverse them, the Scharzhofberg has been tended for the last eight
generations by the Müller family. It is a portrait of a microcosm, where a
pebble dropped into deep water has created widening circles of influence from
a special place looked after by the same family through bad times and good.

The Via Torino in Barbaresco, where the Gaja story first began

Over lunch I probe Gaia about working for her father; he is so disciplined, so passionate that I wonder if sometimes it gets too much for Gaia and her sister, Rossana. 'My father sets a big value on us doing things our own way,' Gaia begins somewhat cautiously. 'He got very cross with me once when I wanted to follow the advice of someone whom I admired. You must find your own way, he tells me. As a result, I've learned so much over the last 15 years. There is no universal truth; you just keep evolving even if that means making mistakes. Finding a new way engages all the team. It is more important to know where you are going than which car you use.' Gaia is warming to her subject and I seem to hear her father's voice echoing in her words. It is time to have a one on one talk with the maestro himself.

We sit opposite each other. If I didn't have to take notes, my eyes would be locked constantly on his. His round red glasses frame his clear blue eyes; his greying hair is swept back to reveal his high forehead. His cupid bow mouth is expressive but rarely still and his strong jaw emphasizes a steely determination. I would have found his intensity to be intimidating a few years ago but I have got to know Angelo a little better; I was recently elected into the same international academy of wine as he and we share some common ground.

We speak French together, French being an official language of Piedmont, and I want to probe him to understand how he rose above the other growers to his position of such standing today. He talks to me about the unique heritage of Barbaresco that he calls '*posizione*' – the Piedmontese equivalent, I think, of 'location, location, location'. He talks about how the individual vineyard sites were the guarantee of a better product; how from the beginning he wanted to harvest ripe Nebbiolo grapes; how the exposure of the vineyard slopes and the heat on the vines was paramount; where here in the Langhe, thanks to Fantini, a 19th-century expert in viticulture, the best southeast and southwest slopes were identified.

He talks about his grandmother Clotilde: 'I was born in 1940 and was 21 years old when she died. I remember her asking me what I wanted to do in life. I stayed silent. She told me that I should become an artisan. It is best to do something with passion. The market does not inspire an artisan. He has his own project in mind, he is proud of it and he knows all of its possibilities in

Angelo Gaia, the maestro

Fiona's favourite Gaja wines

Gaia & Rey Chardonnay

The first thing I notice about this wine is the limestone minerality and intensity that I love in top white wines. Barrel fermented, the presence of French oak is evident but well balanced and pretty, with flavours of orange peel, bergamot, some honeycomb, then flavours that distinguish this wine from a smart white burgundy such as fennel, wild flowers and a touch of hazelnut.

Sorì San Lorenzo

Gaja's greatest single vineyard Barbaresco, the standard bearer of the estate: soft and silky on the attack; lovely nose of ripe fruit, plums, cinnamon, cloves, some sweetness and freshness, great fruit concentration yet ethereal with spicy tannins and balsamic flavours. Elegance and richness combined.

Sorì Tildìn

This wine takes its name from Tilde, the nickname of grandmother Clothilde. The second greatest single vineyard Barbaresco site after San Lorenzo: a generous, warm nose of ripe fruit, warm earth and broad flavours of white chocolate, marzipan, plum and mocha; round smooth tannins and a very pretty acidity which lifts the wine up at the finish.

Darmagi

Gaja's revolutionary Cabernet Sauvignon planted on the Bricco slope next to the family home. Very dark purple, bright and glossy; ripe with earthy, spicy notes with liquorice and black pepper, a touch of Asian spice. Rather like the Chardonnay, this is Cabernet with an Italian take – it is warm, spicy, with aromas that spring out of the glass and intense, grounded tannins.

Sperss

This is my favourite of the two Gaja Barolos from the opposite side of the river near Serralunga. The soils here are limestone and the wine is tarry, intense, brooding and dark on the nose before opening up to reveal dark autumn fruit flavours of sloes and blackberries, minerals and spice. Beautiful intensity.

Egon Müller's celebrated Scharzhofberg vineyards

Riesling, Germany's greatest grape variety, growing in serried ranks

Fiona's tasting book at the Scharzhof

The Scharzberg

Outside the window looms the Scharzberg hill, an undeniable part of the architecture of the estate. I ask Egon if he ever gets tired of looking at it. 'No, not at all,' he laughs. 'It can be stunningly beautiful.' Certainly the 28-hectare site is imposing, seemingly standing on its own in a sea of vines,

Mineral-rich Scharzhofberg soils work magic

and it is a big surface area for a *grand cru* vineyard in Germany. The Egon Müller winery owns 8.5 hectares of the hillside and Egon remembers that when he studied wine at the oenology school in Geisenheim in the mid-1980s, he was the envy of his fellow students since theirs were mainly peasant landholdings in those days.

Many of the vines date back to the beginning of the 20th century, planted with a one metre by one metre high density spacing, which means that all vineyard work needs to be done by hand. Only one or two per cent of these old vines have to be replanted each year. Surprisingly, it is the young vines that often need replanting because they have not settled into the soil well enough to develop a good root system and are therefore more susceptible to the extremes of climate. Unusually for Europe, these are also ungrafted vines (planted before the phylloxera bugs ravaged the vineyards by eating the rootstocks) which is quite risky especially as phylloxera thrives in dry years. Egon admits that in the very hot 2003 vintage: 'I thought that I would have to rip out and replant one parcel. But it is still there. We have very fertile soil with a high amount of organic matter and rainfall is well distributed throughout the year.'

The Scharzhof estate viewed from half way up the Scharzberg

As we walk through the vineyard on a late winter's morning, I kneel down on the hard ground to inspect an old vine. They are beautiful objects, trained on a single pole just as the Romans grew them, wizened and writhing sculptures with gnarly, tactile barks that invite you to touch them to feel their hardened trunks. Egon smiles as if he knows all too well the reverence that an old vine can inspire in a wine lover. 'Since our vines are on their own rootstocks rather than big American ones, our vines look rather tall and skinny,' he comments.

Spring arrives late here and early in the morning before the sun has risen above the hills, the Scharzhofberg is mottled in different shades of grey. Apart from the obvious age of the vines, it is the squeezed-up planting that seems unusual. You might think that this would encourage higher yields per hectare; on the contrary, with closer spacing, the vines have to compete with each other for nutrients and therefore produce fewer grapes. The slate soils play such a magical role: they are rich in minerals but poor in other nutrients, so the grapes ripen very slowly but develop extraordinary intensity. Last year the yields per hectare from this site were a paltry 19 hectolitres per hectare.

It is the steepness of the slope rather than its height that is also striking. The bottom of the hill lies at 200 metres, the top at 311 metres, crowned with a dark tuft of trees like a teenager's quiff. The only time that tractors are used in the vineyard is to winch down the ploughs among the rows. Thanks to the permeability of the slate, the vine roots can dig down deep to anchor themselves, something that I find hard to do myself as I trudge up through these vineyard rows.

Between huffs and puffs, I ask Egon whether he is farming organically. He looks at me quizzically. 'What do you call organic? We only use straw in the vineyards. When it decomposes it binds nitrogen into the soil and helps the soil create organic matter.' None of the marketing speaks about 'bio' wines for Egon; he is one of those unassuming winemakers who seems incredibly humble, as if he can hardly believe his luck in inheriting such a fabulous site.

Egon IV

Born in 1959, Egon grew up in the Scharzhof, went to school locally, studied oenology and joined the winery. Luckily, since his father was in good health, Egon could leave the vineyard to travel to Japan and Australia, to Bordeaux where he worked at Château Pichon-Lalande and to visit importers throughout the world. He hasn't changed much since I met him about 20 years ago, almost bald with an egg shaped head, thick tortoiseshell glasses, a rather bulbous nose and a smile that makes his whole face crease up. There is a sphinx-like character about him: he often smiles as if amused by his own thoughts but dares not share them.

Egon is one of those self-effacing people that you could probably mistake for a maths teacher. He has an air of contentment about him that is very appealing – his wife, Valeska, is a decade or so younger than him (we have previously discovered that it is the same age gap as exists between my husband, Jacques, and me) and he has two teenage children, Egon, aged 18, and Isabelle, aged 15. Even the dog is called Egon, so, as Egon tells it, 'When someone shouts Egon in this house, no one reacts.' Valeska is named after one of Napoleon's lovers and is of French/Polish extraction. She has

Egon's celebrated Scharzhofberger Kabinett Riesling

Egon Müller enjoys a glass of Auslese from his birth year, 1959

Fiona's favourite Egon Müller wines

Scharzhofberger Riesling Kabinett

At first the wine seems rather quiet but then, with a bit of persistence, the aromas of stone fruit, apples and wild herbs are revealed. Instead of an expected sweetness, there is great structure and acidity with lovely inviting freshness and juiciness. With age this wine becomes more expressive and the orchard fruit becomes riper and sweeter, but already in its youth it is showing great balance and purity.

Scharzhofberger Riesling Spätlese

This beautiful wine's flavour is more about being picked at full ripeness than being a late harvest wine. Although this wine could be described as being off dry, the sweetness is not really the point here. What is more important is the abiding depth of fruit and flavour with tastes of white peach and grapefruit. On the palate there are further notes of bergamot and honeydew melon. For all this concentration of fruit and power, the wine still seems light, poised and perfectly balanced.

Scharzhofberger Riesling Auslese

The nose here is sweet and inviting without being cloying. Apricot, peach and melon flavours dance around without settling on the palate. Again the acidity is there with quite surprising austerity but there is a wonderful generosity of flavours and one is given just a glimpse of how this wine is going to develop over the decades to become complete.

Le Gallais, Wiltinger Braune Kupp Riesling Spätlese

The first quality that strikes you about this wine is its crunchy acidity and gorgeous balance between fruit and freshness. It tastes richer and more approachable than the Scharzhofberg wines and yet there is a delicacy to the melon, citrus and peach flavours and a beautiful silky texture that runs over the tongue.

Scharzhofberger Riesling Trockenbeerenauslese

This wine is so rare and so expensive that you approach the glass with reverence. It has a rich, burnished gold colour and a viscous, velvety texture. Yes, there are a lot of sweet pineapple, roasted apricot and peach flavours but above all, amazingly, the acidity is still there, lifting up the sugar and giving great persistence and even energy to this extraordinary wine.

SPRING

Liger-Belair – Burgundy, France

As the vines once again burst into leaf and the vineyard comes to life, Louis Michel Liger-Belair, bristling with pride and success, shows me how he has taken back control of the family vineyards and over the last two decades with minute attention to detail, nurtured them to produce some of the most exciting wines in Burgundy today.

Famille Perrin – Rhône, France

Perrin is the most famous name in southern French winemaking: from the celebrated Château de Beaucastel in Châteauneuf-du-Pape to Angelina and Brad's rosé in Miraval, Provence. This is a portrait of a closely knit family making room for the ambitions and talents of the next generation as the vines once again begin their growing cycle towards ripeness.

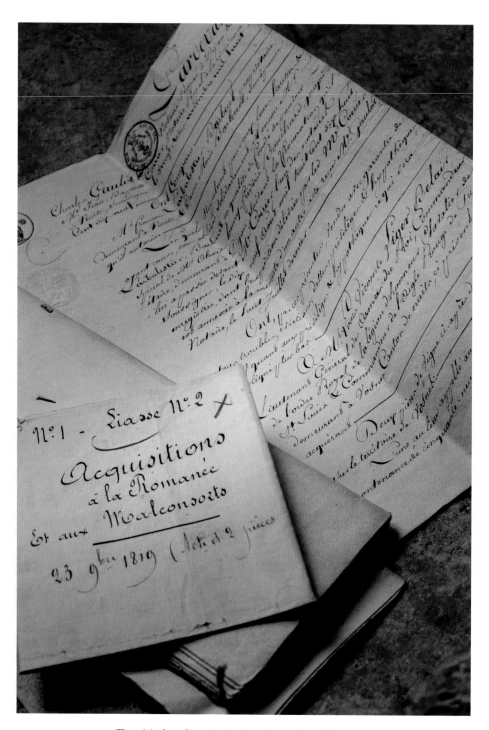

The original parchments attesting to the purchase of vineyards

Liger-Belair

Restoring a grand cru *heritage*

The Battle of Waterloo, 1815. Napoleon is finally defeated and the European continent changes forever. This is also the year when one of Napoleon's generals, Count Louis Liger-Belair, married Claire Cécile Basire in the village of Vosne in the heart of Burgundy's Côte d'Or vineyards. His bride was the widow of General Allemand, one of Liger-Belair's close friends and colleagues. The couple settled in the Basire family home in Vosne where they would live for another two decades and their descendants would live for more than two centuries. Along with the house came some important vineyards including such well-known *grands crus* as La Tâche, La Grande Rue and part of La Romanée.

At this stage, La Romanée was divided into six different parcels and it took some astute bargaining and buying for the general to put the *climat* together until it reached its current size of 84.52 ares, not even one hectare. ('*Climat*' is a Burgundian word that refers to a specific parcel of vines or *cru*; it is a word that I use often when talking about the vineyards of Burgundy.) So began one of the longest ownerships of an estate in Burgundy. Thanks to the hard work and determination of the current heir and occupant of the house, Count Louis-Michel Liger-Belair, the estate has been restored far beyond its former glory and today, for me, represents the greatest, most exciting domaine in the region. It has been quite a roller coaster of a ride.

Family saga

After the French Revolution, when grand families fled and the monasteries – which were by far the largest landowners in the region – were expelled, it was quite easy to pick up land cheaply. Burgundy's vineyards were then, and to a great extent still are, the most erudite wine growing areas in the world. First the Romans and then, around the 10th century, the monasteries settled in the region and began cultivating grapes.

In the Middle Ages, great monasteries run by the Benedictines and the Cistercians such as Cluny, Cîteaux and Vézelay all cultivated their own vineyards in Burgundy. The Cistercian order, which took its name from the nearby abbey of Cîteaux, founded the Clos de Vougeot in 1109 and created Burgundy's largest and most famous walled vineyard. The Cistercian monks were the first to really appreciate the differences in the various plots of land and notice that each parcel gave a slightly different style of wine. They mapped out the first *climats*, laying the foundations for the *cru* system that

Clos de Vougeot is one of the world's most prestigious walled vineyards

should be because of his house, his title and his vineyards. There is a hint of shyness that might account for this too. He is also one of the hardest working vignerons I have ever met.

He met his wife, Constance, about 20 years ago and they married in 1999, a year after Louis-Michel moved into part of the house. She is his anchor, generous and welcoming, throwing the house open to all with good humour, her long brown tresses flowing alongside her open and beautiful face with her clear blue eyes. Constance gives us an hour before supper to explore the vineyards and as storm clouds are gathering we set out to show Alexandre James – who is here for the first time – the hallowed slope of Vosne-Romanée.

We walk through the village, our footsteps echoing off the stone buildings. At 7 o'clock the church bell tolls the angelus just as it does at 7 o'clock in the morning and at midday, and has done for decades. We notice the brass plates of various well-known growers, Méo-Camuzet, Jean Grivot and the world-famous Domaine de la Romanée-Conti. The village looks prosperous, solid and settled, with the church placed firmly in its centre.

The golden slope

We head west along a small road that leads up the gentle slope to an elegant stone cross. This marks the centre of the *grands crus*. On the left are La Tâche and La Grande Rue; on the right the Romanée-Conti vineyard with La Romanée above it and Richebourg off to the side. The dry stone walls that enclose the vineyards have recently been restored as part of the work done to secure a place on the UNESCO World Heritage Site list for the *climats* of the Côte d'Or.

For wine pilgrims this is wine paradise. Wine lovers come from all over the world to visit this revered part of the Côte d'Or, the 'golden slope', which runs from Santenay in the south to Dijon in the north. The slope is divided into the Côte de Beaune mostly to the south of the town of Beaune, with its magnificent Montrachets and Meursaults, and to the north of the town of Nuits-Saint-Georges, the Côte de Nuits, with its majestic red wines such as La

Louis Michel tending his vines   Old vines in bud in the La Romanée vineyard

Romanée, Musigny, Les Bonnes-Mares and Chambertin. One of the factors that makes Burgundy so fascinating to wine lovers is the mosaic of soils and *crus* within 1,250 different *climats* on the Côte d'Or. Louis-Michel adds: '*Terroir* here is not just about the soil. It is about the history of the *climat*, the history of the vine and the history of the man who works the soil.'

I ask Louis-Michel to explain the soils here. Why, for example, is the wine from the bottom part of the slope sold as humble village wine while the *premiers crus* and *grands crus* are found on the hillsides? 'The slope was created 120 million years ago,' he explains. 'It is pure limestone but at the bottom and top of the slope you can find up to 1.20 metres of clay. It is rather like a sandwich: where the limestone is present the *grands crus* are found; they are the meat of the sandwich. On either side where the bread is, the clay is more present.'

We walk up the slope and Louis-Michel points out to us the varying size of pebbles in the soil and we can clearly see the difference between the pebbles of La Romanée and the bigger ones of the *premier cru* of Reignots above it. A lip, like the edge of a stair, separates the two *climats*. The soil of La Romanée is grainier, a mixture of marl and gravel with less clay. 'If the limestone pebbles are not the right size that vineyard will be a *premier cru*; although occasionally the belt of *premiers crus* will open up from time to time to reveal a *grand cru*,' he shows us. La Romanée is one of only two *grand cru* vineyards (the other is Clos de Tart in case you were wondering) planted horizontally to the slope on a north-south axis, so the *climat* is wider rather than taller, to stop erosion. Reignots is unusual in that the *terroir* runs vertically down the slope for 200 metres and encompasses all the different layers of the limestone and clay sandwich. Its wine is rich, full bodied, generous and quite sweet, while La Romanée is more reserved, finer, with black fruit, a beautiful structure, an abiding freshness and smoky reverberation. I served a bottle at a small dinner party not long ago and our guests were speechless; they couldn't find the words to describe the flavours of this wine; all they could talk about was the emotions it inspired. I understood entirely.

At a first glance Burgundy's wines should be quite easy to understand. After all, here in the Côte d'Or, the reds are made from Pinot Noir grapes and the white wines are made from Chardonnay grapes. There are none of the different grape varieties that you find in Bordeaux and the Rhône, and none of the intricate blending techniques needed to bring the various components into a seamless whole. These blends are not necessary in Burgundy since the Pinot Noir is a sort of 'genius grape' – just like Riesling is in Germany and Austria – in that it is able through its nuances of aroma and taste to reflect the place in which it is grown with magnificent precision. Each *climat* on this legendary hillside of Vosne-Romanée is reflected in the way that Pinot Noir tastes when it grown in that specific parcel. For me, this is one of the magical things about burgundy.

I ask Louis-Michel what the risks are here. Hail can be a problem, and with climate change the incidences of hail seem to be more frequent and intense. He also worries about frost. There is a wine growers' saying that this danger is only passed once the Ice Saints – 'Les Saints de Glace', the three saints days of Saint Pancras, Saint Servatus and Saint Mamertus on 11–13 May – have passed. Frost at the beginning of May was a problem in 2016.

Liger-Belair uses horses to work some of these vines. 'The random way that a horse puts his hooves on the soil is important; his foot is heavy but he always places it in a different place. A tractor always uses the same tracks and cannot turn as easily as a horse at the end of the row,' Louis-Michel says, then adds in a typical way, 'but some of the ploughmen are really nuts and that is why I cannot use horses everywhere'.

He farms biodynamically, mixing the field preparations himself, always keeping to the lunar calendar. All of the Vosne producers on this slope use a method called sexual confusion for pest control. This releases pheromones that confuse the insects before they can mate, which means that no insecticides are needed in the area. Butterflies especially are a problem as they can lay their eggs on the grapes and cause them to rot. 'You would expect all the growers here to be organic, but they are not,' he comments, shaking his head sadly and pointing to a parcel of vines, the grass burnt yellow brown by weedkiller and with green moss growing on the vines: 'It's a desert over there.'

Homeward Bound

We walk back through the vine parcels taking the 'Sentier aux Prêtres', the Priests' Way, between Richebourg and La Romanée, used for centuries by the priests crossing over the hillside to say Mass in the next hamlet. The sun is setting behind us and the birdsong increases as long shadows gradually cover the placid waves of the slope, their colour tinted lime green by the new vine shoots. We come back via Les Chaumes, one of the first *climats* bought by the family in 1933. Lower down the hillside on the edge of the village, this *premier cru* produces charming wines with red fruit character and floral notes.

We eat in the kitchen watching Constance as she cooks for us while her husband prepares a fantastic tasting of two great vintages of La Romanée, the 2008 and the 2009. The first vintage is fresher, lighter coloured with cooler but juicier fruit, while the 2009 is richer, more tannic, bigger and riper and garnered much praise and media attention when the wines were first

Horses are used to work the vineyards as their hooves are less destructive than tractor tyres

released. To my surprise, I prefer the 2008, which I think better suits the purity and the energy of Louis-Michel's style of winemaking.

When the pair were first married and came to live here, money was scarce. 'When I first met Constance in 1994, I introduced myself as an impoverished Burgundy peasant,' he recalls. After their marriage, Constance worked for a financial company in Dijon while taking wine tasting courses one day a week. 'I'm not a great taster,' she says humbly, 'but I love the wine'. Louis-Michel's parents always spent half of the year here and his mother, widowed a few years ago, continues the tradition occupying the first floor of the

Louis-Michel at the cross that marks the centre of the Vosne -Romanée *grands cru* vineyards

Louis-Michel's office (top) and the library at the Château de Vosne-Romanée

Constance and Louis-Michel in their kitchen at home

Fiona's favourite Liger-Belair wines

Aux Reignots, Vosne-Romanée Premier Cru

Probably my favourite Liger-Belair wine, as it is always glorious. It has a gorgeous aromatic palette of red fruit, limestone and minerals mixed with floral notes of violets and roses. With age the wine becomes less extrovert but I am always seduced by the silky, glossy texture and the richness that builds up in the mouth.

Vosne-Romanée, Clos du Château Monopole

This walled vineyard lies just in front of the Château de Vosne-Romanée and the soils are made up of denser limestone. The wine is very vibrant with great acidity and easy to appreciate flavours of berries, peonies and violets. For a 'mere' village wine this is a stunner and really quite sophisticated. I love the touch of purity and freshness that you notice right at the end of the finish.

La Romanée, Vosne-Romanée Grand Cru

Majestic is always an adjective that pops up in my tasting notes, although La Romanée wears its greatness elegantly. A seam of beautifully integrated acidity seems to weave together the fruit flavours of summer berries with notes of violets, spice and balsam. There is no stress or tension here, just lovely fruit and minerals as they leave a lasting impression both on the palate and on the mind.

Les Suchots, Vosne-Romanée Premier Cru

Located at the eastern side of the Vosne-Romanée appellation, Les Suchots has more rich clay in its soils and this shows in the wine. The fruit seems more poised and cooler than in the Reignots and there is a fine structure here that delineates the cherry and currant flavoured fruit and also the supple tannic structure. The Pinot Noir grape really shows its true character here with lots of energy and verve.

Clos des Grandes Vignes, Nuits-Saint-Georges Blanc

Tasted for the first time only a couple of years ago, this white wine seems to be giving Louis-Michel so much fun that I expect we will see him making more white wines in the future. The Chardonnay grapes were grafted onto part of the existing vines in 2010 and are still quite young. Yet they have lots of great fruit and floral character, with aromas going from fresh peach and pears to hawthorn blossom and wild flowers. The texture is beautiful and generous and there is lots of charm and depth here. Delicious.

The Perrin family together at the Château de Beaucastel

Since the 16th century, Pierre de Beaucastel's coat of arms has adorned the walls of the drawing room

François and Jean-Pierre in the office they share at Beaucastel

A handsome pair: François Perrin...

The picturesque village of Gigondas

The wilder side of Gigondas with the Dentelles de Montmirail in the distance

his car speakers and we head up a steep, limestone track passing through fields of vines, olives and pine trees. The smell of the pine and the special honey scented *garrigue*, the beautiful late afternoon sunshine, the iconic limestone outcrops that form the Dentelles de Montmirail looming overhead, and the majestic tones of *Parsifal* all combine to make one of those memories that you know will remain with you forever.

We emerge at the top, parcels of vines crisscrossing each other around the circumference of the hilltop. Perrin has bought two hectares of vines up on this clay limestone slope where Syrah is planted. It definitely feels as if we have left the well-mannered Rhône Valley for the wildness of Provence. 'Certainly we haven't bought this to make any money,' Jean-Pierre says with a twinkle in his eye, 'but the heritage is incredible, this is a very special place'. They have already spent five years digging out the hillsides and planting these vines and it will be at least another seven years before they make their first wine. I love the forward thinking dreams of this man in his 70s.

The next morning, we return to take photos with César and are once again entranced by the site. We watch as a horse slowly navigates the terraces to plough up the soil after the winter. It is mesmerizing and reminds me of what Dirk Niepoort once told me about the finest vineyards being in beautiful places. I look forward to tasting the wines from these mountain vines in a decade or so.

Apart from the Clos des Tourelles and the mountain vineyards, the Perrins also have a splendid restaurant with several guestrooms and a wine shop in the centre of the village. Called L'Oustalet, it is a joint venture with Laurent Deconinck, a Belgian chef who grew up in the region. We have the chance to dine there twice during our stay and love the freshness of the local produce cooked perfectly – gastronomic but not fussy. Over dinner we taste some old vintages of Beaucastel: a 1964 which is silky, raisiny with notes of tobacco and liquorice, still incredibly fresh, and a 2000 Hommage that is just coming into its own with very round beautiful dark fruit. The Perrins are so generous with their wines that I find my Moleskine once again filling up with enthusiastic tasting notes and know that I cannot test the reader's patience by transcribing all of them.

Miraval and other family ventures

Château de Beaucastel may be the starting point for the Perrins but it certainly isn't the finishing point. Over the couple of days that we spend with the family, we find out about many of their other ventures. Probably the best known is the joint venture that it still has with Brad Pitt and Angelina Jolie even after the couple's infamous split. The almost 70-hectare property in the South of France is farmed organically and includes vineyards planted with Cinsault, Grenache and Rolle grapes grown exclusively for rosé production. Brad Pitt contacted the Perrin family with the idea of forming a joint venture that would produce and market the wine. The result is the amazingly successful Miraval, which is so pale it hardly looks as if a red grape has passed over its surface.

Jean-Pierre tells me that it is an incredibly technical wine to make, as it needs to be kept as pure as possible, which means no contact with oxygen. The grapes are shipped under nitrogen 120 kilometres to Orange where the Perrins have built a new winery to make the wine. The light colour is exactly what appeals to millennials, who regard it as healthy and pure and untouched by the sun. It is a very pretty wine presented in a champagne style bottle that was especially moulded for Miraval, and I suspect the marketing and the celebrity link make it a veritable cash cow for both partners. I am quite surprised at how serious it is and I have to admit I like drinking it. Rather amusingly, it is Jean-Pierre's hand holding a glass of Miraval that was chosen as the cover photo for the Dutch edition of this book.

The morning we arrive at Beaucastel, François has just landed back from California where he was attending the funeral of Robert Haas of the US importer Vineyard Brands, Perrin Family's importer. Robert had known Jacques Perrin and was close to him. The Haas and Perrin families joined forces to purchase land in Paso Robles, equidistant between San Francisco and Los Angeles. The virgin land where cows had previously grazed was composed of limestone – a rock that potential wine growers are always on the lookout for as it is ideal for growing grapes and olives. The two families took a gamble that they could produce Rhône style wines in the area. The deal risked coming unstuck when the Perrins sent new vines over from Beaucastel. It took three years for the vines to be indexed and certified as virus free and released from customs, so the vineyard was not planted until 1990. The winery there is called Tablas Creek. It is extremely successful and receives 36,000 visitors a year. Today, 150 wineries are established in the Paso Robles region.

The beating heart of the Perrin Family

There is one place that we have yet to see and that is the Perrin Family winery at Grand Prébois on the outskirts of Orange. François lives on one side of the winery and Jean-Pierre on the other. The Miraval rosé is made here as well as the Sélections Parcellaires wines, the Perrin Family Sélection wines, the Gigondas and an entry-level wine called La Vieille Ferme (named after Jean-Pierre's house next door). La Vieille Ferme is a brand that Jean-Pierre started when he joined the company in 1968. He is understandably proud of its success and I ask to be allowed to taste the red wine, which is easy drinking and smooth with typical Rhône flavours – it is also very good value. It is hard to create a branded wine, let alone to develop its growth over 50 years, and I salute the Perrins' winemaking skill as well as their commercial acumen.

The large winery is impressive and acts as a bottling centre, warehouse and dispatch centre for all the wines. It is fairly late in the day, yet the bottling line is still turning, seemingly round the clock, to bottle and package Perrin wines to be sent around the globe. I did not get to see the same facilities at Torres but I am sure that it has a similar sized installation. Beaucastel might be used as the showcase of the family but here is its beating heart.

The money has not just been spent on the latest production line technology. On the other side of the building a glass door etched with the Perrin crest opens onto a magnificent vaulted cellar with sweeping arches and columns worthy of a grand gothic cathedral. Built of high quality concrete with polished floors and subdued lighting, this is a grandiose installation that shows just how important the various Perrin Family projects have become.

There is just one more surprise in store as Jean-Pierre leads us upstairs to a row of light, modern offices. He shows us into an enormous space with five desks. This is the place where the five children involved in sales and marketing – Marc, Thomas, Cécile, Charles and Mathieu – are based in an open plan space where they can bounce ideas off each other. Only César and Pierre, whose duties are on the wine growing and winemaking side, do not have a desk here. I find this wonderful. It is the clearest sign that the vision the two brothers had for their company and for the fifth generation following them is working. 'Everyone has the same sized desk and everyone receives the same salary,' Jean-Pierre adds with a great grin on his face when he sees how awestruck I am.

The brothers have managed to get the family together for our visit, except for Thomas who is in Japan, and Alexandre James is able to take some lovely photos of the clan. The next day, the whole family is gathering for the confirmation of one of Pierre's children and we have been lucky to meet and spend time with them all.

The Perrin Family's cathedral-like new wine cellar at Orange

Conclusion

The wine world has seen a huge change over the last 20 or so years and many of the stories I have told here concern the fourth or fifth generation of a family who until recently were just content to be wine farmers. But the wine business has gone global thanks to the internet, and a new world has opened up which includes wealthy wine drinkers, worldwide fame and the sort of celebrity status which used to be accorded to film stars, sportsmen and women and Michelin starred chefs.

Wine has become both democratized and elitist. We have never been so well informed about wine nor has it been so accessible: competitions, promotions, scores, blogs, books and reviews abound. At the other end of the scale, the top wines which were until recently the privilege of royalty, Oxbridge colleges, seats of government and embassies and the occasional fanatical collector, are now offered to a select group of extremely rich wine lovers through winemaker-hosted dinners and gala parties at selected domaines and châteaux. Great wines, produced in small quantities by well-known winemakers, have become luxury products and now command stratospheric prices.

The gap between the 'blue chip' wines purchased either for investment, status bragging rights or pure drinking pleasure and the average wine purchased for everyday drinking can be over €1,000. There is more motivation to succeed in the wine business today, and where a couple of generations ago famous wine producers' children were heading for the cities to find a different career, it is with pride that today's generations take on their parents' mantles knowing they can fulfil their ambitions. The oenology schools and viticulture colleges have never been so full.

What makes the difference between a family-run and a corporate-run winery? Can you taste it in the glass? Maybe not, but the person behind the label is as important to the wine lover as the taste of the wine, and when that person comes from a family tradition rooted in a vineyard with a taste of its own, there is a more emotional involvement – especially if those traditions go back several generations. That person is an integral part of the *terroir* or the sense of place, that makes a vineyard so special.

Many families regard their role as being guardians of the land that they were lucky to inherit and did not have to pay for; they feel that they are its custodians, at least for their generation. As my husband, Jacques, says about the 400-year old family house that we live in: 'We are just the current link in a very long chain.' The present generation want to build on that inheritance and leave their mark for the future generations to follow. To do this, they need to take a very long-term view and have enough capital and resources to weather the storms. Being able to manage family members and their expectations is of paramount importance. Apart perhaps from a luxury car, a beautiful jacket or a fine wristwatch, most winemakers are not flashy or showy and their usual uniform is jeans.

Keeping a family together is not easy. Harvard Business School estimates that 70% of family businesses are sold or taken over before the second generation and only 12% survives to the third. There is a saying that the first generation creates, the second generation profits and the third generation sells. Having read this far, you will probably have sensed the undercurrents of tensions present in many of the stories I tell.

On their request and also because it serves no one, least of all the wine lover, I have often skirted around the murkier details of family struggles. Sometimes families can be so belligerent that their disagreements can ruin their family vineyards; a stark example of this is the great Mondavi family who, by the third generation, had to sell out in the 1980s to a major drinks corporation.

To all of the other skills needed to run a family business, patience and diplomacy have to be added. With vineyards now fetching such enormous sums (*grand cru* Burgundy land is up to almost €50 million a hectare) the temptation to sell is intense, especially when other family members not active in the business want out. In France, the Napoleonic Code decrees that all inheritance should be equally divided between the heirs, male and female, and has caused the division of many estates.

I am full of admiration for the 10 families I have chosen to profile in this book and I hope that their domaines will still be run by them for generations to come. Their stories may be quite different but the thread that binds them together is the vision, hard work and determination needed to run their estates well.

Apart from the high financial stakes that money has brought to the wine business, probably the greatest menace these families face today is that of climate change, with increasingly violent weather bringing serious risks of hail, spring frosts, warmer temperatures and summer drought. Higher alcohol levels caused by higher temperatures are threatening the natural balance in wines and making them difficult to drink, let alone age. Precious grape varieties that families have cultivated for centuries may not be suitable to grow in their vineyards in the future. Spare a thought for all of them in the years to come, and when you have the chance to enjoy one of their wines, pause for a moment to think of all the history, culture and tenacity that have gone into that glass.

Fiona Morrison MW

To my husband Jacques, with whom I share my life in wine, and to all my family, who are my inspiration

Published 2019 by Académie du Vin Library Ltd.
www.academieduvinlibrary.com

Editor: Susan Keevil
Designer: Aurélie Matthys
Photography by Alexandre James Rocca-Serra
(photographs pp 55, 57 Andrew Verschetze)

ISBN: 978-1-913141-01-1